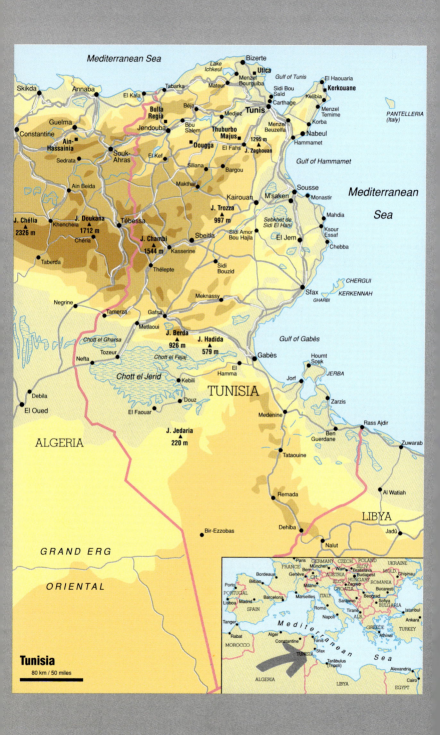

INSIGHT POCKET GUIDE

TUNISIA

APA PUBLICATIONS
Part of the Langenscheidt Publishing Group

Welcome!

This guidebook combines the interests and enthusiasms of two of the world's best-known information providers: Insight guides, who have set the standard for visual travel guides since 1970, and Discovery Channel, the world's premier source of non-fiction television programming.

Its aim is to help visitors to Tunisia make the best use of limited time. Purposely selective but intent on reflecting the country's surprising diversity, the author, Dorothy Stannard, has devised a series of itineraries grouped around five key bases (Tunis, The Northwest, Sousse, the Oases, and Jerba and the Ksour). They take visitors from mysterious medinas to showcase resorts, from hot springs to a world-class museum, from a fabled synagogue to Berber strongholds, and from lush palmeries to crystallised salt lakes.

Distances are short and it is possible to sample each of the bases within the space of two weeks. Visitors with less time should be governed by taste and season – the Oases and the Ksour in winter, the Northwest, Tunis and Sousse in summer.

 On **Dorothy Stannard's** first trip to Tunisia she didn't expect to be enchanted: 'Used to the flamboyance of Egypt and the intensity of Morocco, I expected a paler version of these – less challenging, more packaged, somewhere to extend a beach towel rather than the mind.'

But Tunisia proved persuasive, and its colours and shapes – curving window grilles, stark white domes and gorgeously patterned tiles – illuminated her winter memories. In spring, she combined a tour of the Roman ruins of the Tell with forays to the wild beaches of Cap Bon and the north. 'These remain two of my favourite places,' she says, 'but other places tug: the holy city of Kairouan, the palm oases of Tozeur and Nefta, the desert ksours and the island of Jerba in the Gulf of Gabes.'

C O N T E N T S

*Pages 2/3:
Chott el
Guettar*

Pages 8/9: In Kairouan's Mosque of the Barber

HÍSTORY &

Venture behind Tunisia's glossy east coast facade of uniform hotels and beaches and you lift the lid on its past. Out pop astonishing riches: Arab spices, Moorish doorways, Berber colours, Turkish pastries, Saharan tattoos, French railways – the sizeable legacy of a long line of immigrants and invaders. For most visitors the chief surprise is the wealth of classical ruins, crowned – in terms of historic resonance if not in the quality of the remains – by the ancient city of Carthage, hub of the mighty Carthaginian empire and later rebuilt by Rome. Many of these ruins still enjoy the kind of semi-wild settings beloved of 18th-century landscape artists.

A Woman of Substance

The founding of Carthage is put at around 800BC and attributed, in myth at least, to Queen Dido, a refugee from the Phoenician city of Tyre. According to legend, the local chieftain, Iarbus, agreed to give the Queen and her entourage as much land as could be covered by an ox hide. Undeterred by such parsimony, the resourceful Dido had the hide of the largest ox cut into the thinnest of strips and strung around the hill of Byrsa (a Greek word for hide), a neat piece of out-manoeuvring that added grist to the creative mill for both Virgil (*The Aeneid*) and Henry Purcell (*Dido and Aeneas*).

The settlement was the start of Carthage (Qart Hadasht: New Capital), a great maritime and commercial power that dominated the Mediterranean for 700 years. Until the rise of Rome, its only equal was Greece.

Mosaic of the goddess Tanit

CULTURE

Because of the subsequent razing of Punic Carthage, knowledge about the Carthaginian people is sketchy. They are known to have been skilled plumbers (witness the well-appointed bathrooms at Kerkouane on Cap Bon) and to have worshipped the gods Tanit and Baal. They are remembered most, though, for sacrificing their children (*see page 30*), a measure taken only *in extremis* (war or pestilence) to appease the gods, but seized upon as evidence of gross barbarity by the rising power on the other side of the Mediterranean: Rome.

Carthage Versus Rome

Conflict between Carthage and Rome – the Mediterranean was not big enough for both of them – erupted in a series of wars known as the Punic Wars. The First Punic War broke out over Sicily in 263 BC and was won by Rome after a series of skirmishes lasting 20 years. The Second Punic War (218–201 BC) was also won by the Romans, though the odds closed when the famous Carthaginian general Hannibal trekked through Spain and the Alps on elephants to attack Rome from the rear. The Third Punic War, a three-year siege of Carthage (149–146 BC), fulfilled Cato's fervent wish and warcry: '*Delenda est Cartago*' (Carthage must be destroyed).

Carthage was razed and salt was ploughed into its soil to prevent a

Hannibal and elephants cross the Alps

resurrection. But eventually, as Roman influence expanded in North Africa, the Romans rebuilt the ancient city for their own use, and it is the Roman remains that survive today.

North Africa was Rome's pantry. It was the grain-bin of the Empire and a bottomless well of olive oil – at El Jem alone Hadrian ordered the planting of 37,000 acres/15,000 hectares of olive groves. It also supplied wild animals for the empire's amphitheatres. War veterans were settled here, and towns such as Thugga (now Dougga), Bulla Regia, Thysdrus (now El Jem), Makhtar and Sbeitla flourished, as the remains of their sumptuous villas, temples and mosaics show.

The eventual decline of the Roman Empire opened the door to the Vandals, who set about wrecking everything that the Romans had achieved. The smashed noses of Roman busts now in the Bardo museum were just the tip of their destructive handiwork. The devastation was partially reversed in the 6th century when Emperor Justinian of the Eastern (Byzantine) Empire vanquished the Vandals and set about rebuilding. But salvage was only temporary. By the next century a new conqueror was rearing in the east: the Arabs under the rousing banner of Islam. Their leader was Oqba Ibn Nafaa and their purpose was to spread the new faith *besiff* (by the sword).

The Arab Conquest

It wasn't until Oqba Ibn Nafaa's third incursion into Tunisia in 670 that he founded Kairouan. Though myth attributes his choice of such a seemingly unpropitious and arid site to divine signs – a spring reputedly connected to the holy well of Zem Zem in Mecca and the miraculous appearance of a golden goblet – it was clearly dictated by logic. Arab strength was in land-based combat, and the site was on caravan (hence Kairouan) routes midway between their two main opponents: the Byzantines on the coast and the Berbers in the hills. Building materials for the new city – columns and blocks of stone – were plundered from the abandoned Roman towns.

Roman mosaic depicting Tunisian fishermen

To begin with, allegiance was paid to Baghdad, but in the 8th century the settlers sought autonomy under Ibrahim ben el Aghlab, a local leader, who promised the caliph an annual tribute in return for virtual independence. Thus began a century of Aghlabid rule and the Golden Age of Kairouan.

By 863 Kairouan had the Great Mosque that you see today, which doubled as a fortress, and was a centre of religious doctrine, crafts and poetry. The Aghlabid palaces, built outside the city away from the wrathful theologians, were dedicated to indulgence, fulfilling every Western fantasy of opulent furnishings, bosky gardens, tinkling fountains and gauze-clad slaves bearing sherbet. Trade boomed on the back of the trans-Saharan traffic in slaves and gold, which Kairouan merchants supplied to Sfax, Sousse and the growing town of Tunis.

Kairouan, on the caravan trail

Until then the Berbers, the indigenous people of the whole of North Africa, had dealt with invaders by launching intermittent but violent raids. This time, however, they embraced the new religion of Islam, which suited their temperament, and joined *jihads* (holy wars) into Sudan and Europe. In 740 they formed the Kharijite sect, a fiercely puritanical brand of Islam, which rebelled against the Orthodox mainstream. It was eventually put down, though pockets of Kharijites survive to this day, notably on Jerba.

Unlike their counterparts in Morocco and Algeria, the tribes in Tunisia had few high mountains in which to hide, so from quite early on they integrated with the Arab population. Today, distinctions between Arabs and Berbers are blurred and the Berber language has died out. Social divides are primarily rural/urban rather than Berber/Arab.

Trade Favours Tunis

When the Aghlabid dynasty foundered, Kairouan declined. Mahdia, south of Sousse, became the capital of the Fatimids (910–969), whose empire spread all the way to Egypt, and the Hafsids (1230–1574) based themselves in Tunis, which was better placed to exploit trade opportunities with Europe. Other northern ports also expanded and El Mustansir commissioned a magnificent hunting park on the shores of Lake Ichkeul near Bizerte.

From the late 15th century the Maghreb received Muslims and Jews chased out of Spain by the Inquisition. When the Spanish

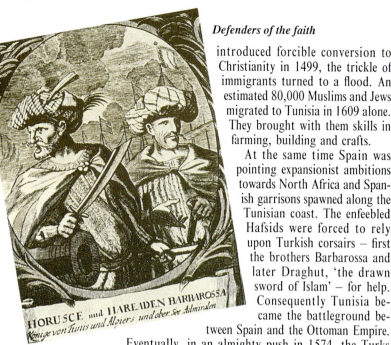

HORUSCE und HAREADEN BARBAROSSA
Könige von Tunis und Algiers und ober See Admiralen

introduced forcible conversion to Christianity in 1499, the trickle of immigrants turned to a flood. An estimated 80,000 Muslims and Jews migrated to Tunisia in 1609 alone. They brought with them skills in farming, building and crafts.

At the same time Spain was pointing expansionist ambitions towards North Africa and Spanish garrisons spawned along the Tunisian coast. The enfeebled Hafsids were forced to rely upon Turkish corsairs – first the brothers Barbarossa and later Draghut, 'the drawn sword of Islam' – for help. Consequently Tunisia became the battleground between Spain and the Ottoman Empire. Eventually, in an almighty push in 1574, the Turks ousted the Spanish and Tunisia was absorbed by the Empire.

The resulting Turkish influence is most marked in Tunis, especially in the vicinity of the medina's Zitouna Mosque. Surrounding mosques and *zaouias* (centres of religious cults) sport the octagonal, Turkish-style minaret rather than the square Maghrebi-style which tops the far earlier (Aghlabid) Zitouna. The souks are full of Turkish flourishes, from barley-sugar columns in red, gold and green to the pastel facades of the *bijoutiers*, gorgeously adorned with arabesques and sensuously entwined flowers and twirls. The Turks also introduced their coffee – thick and sweet in tiny cups – along with honey-soaked pastries, red fezzes and hubble-bubble pipes.

Government was placed in the hands of a pasha, appointed by the emperor in Constantinople, who devolved responsibility to beys, in charge of civil matters and finance, and deys, senior army officers. As time went on, however, Tunisia enjoyed virtual independence from Turkey.

A French Protectorate

Meanwhile European interest in Tunisia was increasing. Foreign loans helped the economy and a new law in 1857 gave non-Muslims equal legal status and the right to own land. Ahmed Bey (ruled 1837–54) actively courted European approval, hanging pictures of Napoleon in his palace and reorganising the army along European lines. When, therefore, the future of the crumbling Ottoman Empire came under review at the 1878 Congress of Berlin, Tunisia was eyed with interest, especially by the Italians and the French.

In the end, it was the French who got the prize. A cattle-rustling raid into Algeria by Khroumirian tribesmen gave them the pretext to move in (Algeria had been a French colony since 1830), and in 1883 the Treaty of Bardo formalised Tunisia's new status as a French protectorate.

The new regime built roads and railways, developed agriculture, including reviving a long-dormant viticulture, and launched new industries, in particular phosphate mining. A minimum standard of health care was laid down. Many Tunisian men and women adopted European dress. To begin with, opposition to French presence centred on the Young Tunisians, who modelled themselves on the Young Turks. They were drawn from the upper-middle class – nearly all of them were educated at the esteemed Sadiki College in Tunis – and preferred to take an intellectual approach to nationalism rather than a hands-on, take-to-the-streets course. The group evolved into the Destour Party in 1920.

It wasn't until Habib Bourguiba came along that the party found a popular voice. Bourguiba, educated at the Lycée Carnot in Tunis and then in Paris, knew how to harness discontent. Even though he was Europeanised and had a French wife (and later tried to force through 'progressive' reforms), he roused popular indignation at the eclipse of Tunisian mores, language and dress.

To forward his aims, he formed the Neo-Destour Party in 1934 and became a full-time political activist. His party was illegal for 20 years, and he was frequently under house arrest or in prison. It was a long, hard road to independence, menaced by terrorists on both sides in the form of the nationalist Fellagha guerrillas and the *colons'* Red Hand.

Bourguiba's Vision

Independence was granted on 20 March 1956. Shortly afterwards Bourguiba became president, a post he held for 31 years. His achievements were many – universal education, big improvements in health care, advances in industry and the abolition of polygamy. Women were given equal civil rights. Cap Bon and Sousse-Monastir were targeted for massive tourist expansion, and in the mid-1970s developers built Port el Kantaoui, a self-contained sanitised version of Tunisia with 'Andalusian'-style apartments, a marina, shops and restaurants, and polite reminders to take your litter with you and keep off the grass.

But Bourguiba came perilously close to be-

Habib Bourguiba

Pictures of Ben Ali

ing a despot, especially during later years of his presidency when his grip began to slip. From the start, all opposition was suppressed, the media was controlled and there were the usual attempts to build a personality cult: portraits in public places, grandiose statues, and the re-naming of main boulevards and streets after him. In 1974 Bourguiba was elected 'president for life'.

But this time he had ignored the public mood. His vision of a modern, secular Tunisia failed to take full account of the importance of tradition and religion to the ordinary man-in-the-kasbah.

In 1987, at the grand old age of 84, seven doctors certified Bourguiba as senile and unfit to rule. He was succeeded by his prime minister, Zine al-Abidine Ben Ali on 7 November 1987. On taking power, Ben Ali instituted various reforms and made tentative moves away from a one-party state. Within two years, 10,000 of Bourguiba's political opponents were released from jail.

Since then, Ben Ali has had to steer a difficult course between introducing reforms and ensuring that the terrible fundamentalist violence that has gripped neighbouring Algeria cannot take hold in Tunisia. In 1994 changes in the electoral law continued a gradual process of increased democratisation, allowing some seats in the Chamber of Deputies (the Tunisian Parliament) to be allocated on a proportional representation basis (previously all seats in each multi-member constituency went to the party that received the most votes – in effect the RCD party).

Presidential and parliamentary elections were held during that year and Ben Ali stood for a second term of office. He was duly elected as president. In the parliamentary elections opposition parties secured 19 seats in the Chamber of Deputies. In 1999 Ali won a third term, while opposition party seats in parliament rose to 20 percent. Bourguiba died peacefully at home in 2000.

Economic Climate

The country's economy is fairly stable, though it takes a downturn every time there is a drought) and the country's infrastucture is constantly being improved.

The country's biggest exports are textiles, agricultural products, petroleum, phosphates and olive oil; its chief imports are foodstuffs to feed its escalating population, which is currently around 9.5 million.

Tradition and tourism

Historical Highlights

1000BC Phoenician traders establish ports along the North African coast.

814BC The founding of Carthage.

700–409BC Conflict between Carthage and Greece over spheres of influence and trade routes. Child sacrifice is stepped up in an appeal to gods Tanit and Baal.

263BC Antagonism between Rome and Carthage. The First Punic War is triggered by a dispute over Sicily.

218–201BC The Second Punic War. Hannibal crosses the Alps.

146BC The Third Punic War ends in Carthage falling to Rome.

1st and 2nd century AD Period of Roman expansion. New towns are founded, often on the remains of old Punic settlements.

3rd century Christianity spreads throughout Roman North Africa. Mosaics acquire Christian themes.

429 Invasion by the Vandals.

534 Byzantines oust the Vandals and try to recover control.

647–670 The Arabs defeat the Byzantines and introduce Islam. Oqba Ibn Nafaa founds Kairouan. Authority rests with the eastern caliphs.

8th century Kharijitism spreads among the Berbers.

800–909 The Aghlabid dynasty quells Kharijite zeal and ushers in the Golden Age of Kairouan.

910–969 The Fatimid dynasty rules from Mahdia. In 969 it moves its base to Cairo.

1148 Roger II of Sicily acquires Jerba, Mahdia, Gabes and Sfax.

1159–1230 The Christians are expelled by the Almohads whose brief but effective rule of the Maghreb is directed from Marrakesh.

1230–1574 The Hafsid dynasty. The capital moves to Tunis, which attracts increasing numbers of European merchants.

1270 Aborted crusade to Tunisia by Louis IX of France.

1332 The Arab historian Ibn Khaldoun is born in Tunis.

1492 Muslim and Jewish migration from Spain culminates with the fall of Muslim Granada. The newcomers bring much-needed skills in agriculture and crafts.

1534–81 Tunisia is a pawn in struggles between Spain and Turkey, and in 1574 is sucked into the Ottoman Empire.

17th century Piracy reaches its peak in the Mediterranean.

1705–1881 Period of the Husseinite Beys. Turkey's authority is nominal. New mosques and *medersa* (lodging houses for students) are built, especially in Tunis. Foreign loans are raised to help stem the haemorrhage in the treasury.

1881 The French invade under the pretext of pacifying tribes living on the border with Algeria.

1883 The Treaty of Bardo formally establishes Tunisia's status as a French protectorate.

1934 Resistance centres on the Neo-Destour Party, founded by Habib Bourguiba.

1942–1943 The Tunisia Campaign of World War II. Tunisia witnesses some of the fiercest fighting of the Desert War.

1956–1957 Independence is granted. Bourguiba becomes president. The Code of Personal Status is introduced, outlawing polygamy and giving Tunisian women equal civil rights to men.

1987 Bourguiba is ousted in a coup on grounds of senility. Ben Ali becomes president. Thousands of political prisoners are released from jail.

1992 Wary of growing Islamic violence in neighbouring Algeria, Ben Ali's government cracks down on fundamentalism.

1994 Presidential and parliamentary elections. Ben Ali wins second term in office.

1999 In October, Ben Ali wins a third term in government. Opposition seats in the Chamber of Deputies increase to 20 percent.

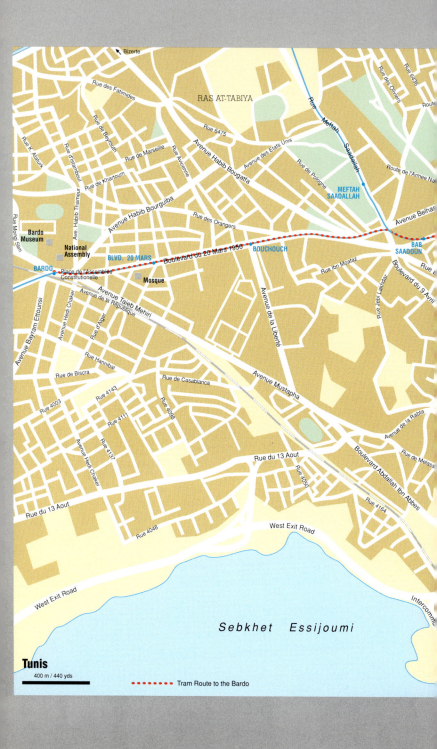

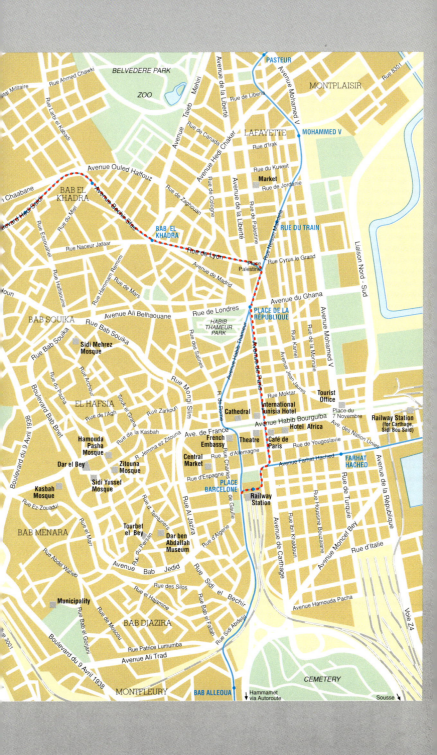

In terms of tourism, Tunisia's capital is less celebrated than the coastal cities to the south: its image is workaday rather than holiday. But for the independent traveller, either with a car or prepared to hop on local buses and trains, Tunis makes an ideal base. An hour's drive in almost any direction leads to the country's best attractions: fine sands, idyllic rural backwaters, Roman ruins, Lake Ichkeul or Hammamet, the most appealing of the big resorts. Closer still are the remains of Ancient Carthage and the hill-top village of Sidi Bou Saïd, both easily reached on the light railway from Avenue Habib Bourguiba.

Tunis evolved into a city under the Arabs. In the 9th century the Aghlabids finished the Zitouna Mosque (the Great Mosque) and in the 13th century the Hafsids made the expanding city their capital.

The city itself can be recommended for its medina, where refined Turkish influences still linger in octagonal minarets, traditional cafés and shopfronts; a good choice of restaurants; inexpensive but well-run hotels and the Bardo Museum with its superb collection of Roman mosaics. What's more, though Tunis lacks the grandeur of other capitals, it still flaunts big-city confidence and style. This makes a refreshing change from much of the rest of the country, which is either agrarian (and therefore largely poor), in thrall to tourism or so hell-bent on the extraction of phosphates or oil that cultural interests are ignored.

Tunis: Avenue Habib Bourguiba and cathedral

Medina tiles

1. The Medina

A full day in Tunis. A walking tour of the medina (map overleaf) to see the Tourbet el Bey and the souks; lunch in the shadow of the Zitouna Mosque. Afternoon in the Bardo Museum.

This is a long day, so an early start and robust walking shoes are essential. If you plan to spend more than one day in Tunis then you can set a more leisurely pace and split this itinerary into two tours, spending one day in the medina and the other at the Bardo (note: the Bardo is closed on Monday). An ideal way to end a long day in the city is to take yourself off to a hammam *(Turkish bath) for an invigorating steam.*

Begin with a fortifying coffee on the terrace of **Café de Paris** on **Avenue Habib Bourguiba**, the bushy spine linking Place du 7 Novembre and the entrance to the medina. As most Tunis cafés are stand-up affairs in the mode of Italian *espresso* bars, outside tables at the Café de Paris are at a premium. You will need to be quick off the mark to secure one before the well-practised locals.

On the Avenue

Afterwards turn left along the pedestrianised centre of the Avenue, where florists will be hosing down the

21

pavements and putting the finishing touches to bridal displays.

Bright with flowers, cool, and invariably filled with birdsong, the avenue is undeniably pleasant. Among the flanking buildings are several relics from colonial days, including the French-built theatre, the French Embassy and the Catholic cathedral, the latter two facing one another across a statue of Ibn Khaldoun, the 14th-century Tunis-born historian. At this point the avenue becomes **Avenue de France**, thick with market stalls, shoeshines and 'plastification' booths. This ends at Place de la Victoire and the Bab el Bahar, a marooned Hafsid gate marking the entrance to the medina, which are both overlooked by the blue *mashrabiya* balconies of the British Embassy.

From here several narrow alleyways strike into the medina. Take **Rue Jemaa ez Zitouna**, the main drag, leading to the Zitouna Mosque. It is packed with souvenir shops, but in between the leather jackets, toy camels and brass trays you will find a few shops supplying local needs. Deeper in the medina, particularly around the Zitouna Mosque, goods and trades separate into their own souks according to the medieval guild pattern. Divisions are not as strict as they once were, however; gold and jewellery shops, for example, swamp most of the streets behind the Zitouna Mosque, including Souk de la Laine (wool).

The route, overhung by blue wooden porches and balconies, climbs steadily. Just before the Zitouna it enters a long, covered arch lined with yet more shops. Come back to this spot later. First,

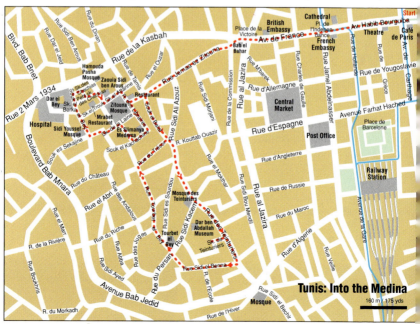

Tunis: Into the Medina

160 m / 175 yds

turn left just before the arch, down **Souk el Balat** (the place to buy *makrouth*, sticky pastries filled with date or fig paste), for a look at local commerce and to see the Tourbet el Bey, the mausoleum of the Husaynid dynasty. Its quiet upper reaches yield to a lively market, a mixture of traditional apothecaries and food stalls punctuated by red and green 'barber pole' pillars – Turkish touches that recur in the medina.

At the end of the market, branch right into **Rue des Teinturiers** and, where the road forks, bear left into what is ostensibly Rue Dar ben Abdallah but which later resumes the name Rue des Teinturiers (the right-hand route is Rue Sidi es Sourdou). The octagonal minaret belongs to the **Mosque des Teinturiers**, otherwise known as Mosque Jdid ('the New'), one of several lavish buildings commissioned during the mid-18th-century trade boom.

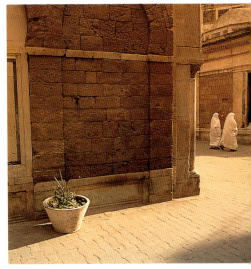

The Tourbet el Bey

On the right a little way past the mosque, look out for an arrow pointing to **Dar ben Abdallah** (Tues–Sun 9.30am–4.30pm, closed Mon; admission fee), a palatial town-house converted into a museum depicting the 'daily life of Tunis in the 19th century'. If you plan to cover only the medina today and haven't lingered too long on Rue Jemaa ez Zitouna, then have a quick look inside. An old map of the medina inside the museum's entrance pinpoints the medina's *hammams*, worth noting if you want to indulge in a relaxing post-tour steam.

Back on Rue des Teinturiers, a pungent alleyway a little further along on the right is the **Petit Souk des Teinturiers**, the dwindled remnants of the dyeing industry, usually signalled by skeins of newly dipped wool. Just past here Rue des Teinturiers enters a series of markets. Before the fish stalls, strike right up Rue Sidi el Benna, a quiet residential street notable only for its studded doors and rusty wrought-ironwork. A right turn at the top will bring you out on Rue Tourbet el Bey which leads back towards the Zitouna Mosque via the extensive mausoleum of the Husaynid beys.

The **Tourbet el Bey** (mausoleum) (Tues–Sun 9.30am–4pm, closed Mon; admission fee) is impossible to miss; look out for its green domes. It was restored under the auspices of l'Association de Sauvegarde de la Medina and is now open to visitors. The Husaynids ruled Tunisia from the 18th century until independence in 1957. Their mausoleum was built by Ali Pasha II in the mid-18th century.

Zitouna Mosque

Each of the tiled chambers is crammed with tombs, their headstones topped by marble turbans or fezzes in the Turkish style.

Continuing along Rue Tourbet el Bey, you pass a small mosque (No 41) where Ibn Khaldoun studied, and the house (No 33) where he was born in 1332. To regain the point where you left Rue Jemaa ez Zitouna, turn right down Rue du Trésor and then left, retracing your steps back down Souk el Balat.

Back on Rue Jemaa ez Zitouna, pass through the covered archway to the Zitouna Mosque. On the way, note the unnamed restaurant on the right inside the arch (my recommendation for lunch); by now (a little after 11am) its staff will probably be grappling with an enormous tuna.

The **Zitouna** (olive tree) **Mosque** (Sat–Thurs, winter 8am–1pm, summer 8am–7pm, closed Fri; admission fee) is the Great Mosque, the physical and spiritual heart of the medina and the centre of theological studies right up until the 1960s, when ex-President Bourguiba transferred Islamic studies to the city's university in an attempt to curb the *imams'* influence. The Omayyads initiated the building of a mosque on this spot in the 8th century, but it was the Aghlabids in the 9th century who completed the structure, which at that time was a third of the size of the Great Mosque in Kairouan, their capital. Due to embellishments and renovation over the centuries, only the prayer hall is little changed. Like the Great Mosque in Kairouan, it incorporates a forest of Roman columns removed from archaeological sites. Unfortunately, only a few of these can be seen by non-Muslims, who are restricted to the viewing platform overlooking the stone *sahn* (courtyard).

As you leave through the mosque's door, cross the balcony and look up to the left to glimpse the roof terrace of the Musée de Bonheur, where scraps of Roman friezes and columns have been wedded to Arab tilework in a mock Arab-Roman ruin. Such terraces crown the carpet and souvenir shops hereabouts. Needless to say, they serve as bait to lure potential carpet-buying customers, but are good for roof-top views nevertheless.

Out of the mosque, turn right then slightly left and immediately right into Rue des Librairies, where there are several *medersa*, lodging-houses-cum-schools for the theological students who studied at the mosque. The **Palm Tree Medersa** (1714) is immediately on the right, marked by a yellow studded door; the **Bachiya Medersa** (1752) is opposite a makeshift café and *hammam* and **Es Slimanya Medersa** (1754) is on the corner of Rue des Librairies and Rue de la Medersa Slimanya. Only the Slimanya is open to the public (same ticket as the Zitouna Mosque). Visitors can see the courtyard and, for an additional small charge, the interior of the old mosque. This *medersa* was commissioned by Ali Pasha to commemorate the burial of his son.

Proceed up Rue de la Medersa Slimanya and through two green doors to Souk el Kachachine. Go right at **Souk des Femmes** (women), the third alleyway on the right, where Tunis matrons bargain over the white or cream fabric for their *haik* (cover-all) and tailors labour over antiquated sewing-machines. Turn left at **Souk de la Laine** (wool), now mainly jewellery shops, and at the end of here turn right into an unnamed souk (you should see a keyhole arch up ahead). Turn left at **Souk el Leffa**, noted for carpets, and then take the second right through two green doors into a large jewellery souk (a shop opposite the doors offers a *terrasse panoramique*). The lovely pastel facades of these shops are painted with Arab/Turkish designs: exquisite jewel-boxes for the gems they contain.

After a few paces the route crosses **Souk el Berka**, a small vaulted place supported by green and red striped pillars, which was formerly the site of the old slave market. Captives taken from black Africa and Christian victims of Barbary Coast piracy were auctioned here until 1841, when Ahmed Bey closed the market and outlawed slavery in an attempt to win the approval of European leaders (his bankruptcy ensued).

The route then passes into a wider, trellis-covered thoroughfare, again devoted to jewellers. Look out for the booth where gold is taken to be weighed and valued; the price of any gold item is determined by current gold prices plus a little extra for the work.

Peep down Rue Sidi ben Ziad on the left shortly past the souk for a glimpse of another octagonal minaret, this time of the Sidi Youssef Mosque, built by Youssef Dey in 1616 to serve the Ottoman troops. Carry on through a pair of blue doors and you enter **Souk el Bey**, flanked on the left by the back of the Dar el Bey, the former beylical palace and now housing the offices of the prime minister and the ministry of foreign affairs – moved here from the nouvelle ville in an attempt to restore political status to the medina in the wake of independence. Take the

Bargain hard!

Downstairs in Mrabet

second pair of doors on the right-hand side of Souk el Bey to enter the vaulted **Souk des Chechias**, devoted to the red fezzes beloved by elderly city gents. With its high vaulted ceilings, gilt mirrors and arabesque flourishes, this is one of the most atmospheric spots in the medina. Each outlet off the shadowy souk is a shop-cum-work-shop with a wooden counter for sales and a group of intent crafts-men busy shaping, trimming and raising the nap of the felt with teazle brushes. At one time this souk supplied cities all over North Africa and the Middle East. Sadly, each year business seems slacker and some of the booths are now disused.

The souk is intersected by a long café (originally a street) linked to the **Petit Souk des Chechias**, which runs parallel. The café, fra-grant with Turkish coffee and decorated with murals, is a favourite spot for businessmen and hat-makers alike. Stop off for a *café Turc* or a *Boga* (lemonade) and a puff on a hubble-bubble pipe, another pleasure introduced by the Turks. The weed is simple tobacco, though the relaxing effect often leads novices to suspect something stronger. You can order a full or half measure.

By now it is probably time to return to the Zitouna Mosque for lunch at the restaurant I pointed out earlier. To get there, proceed to the bottom of Petit Souk des Chechias, which emerges bang in front of the 17th-cen-tury Hamouda Pasha Mosque on Rue Sidi ben Arous. Turn right and head towards the square minaret (Maghrebi rather than Turkish) of the Zi-touna, passing on your left the green doors of the Zaouia of Sidi

Felt fezzes

ben Arous, an important Sufi mystic. At the end of Rue Sidi ben Arous, turn left into the thriving **Souk el Attarine** (perfume). You can order your own tailor-made scent here or have internationally famous perfumes, such as Chanel No 19, Poison and Kouros, replicated. The souk emerges beside the Zitouna Mosque. Walk past the front of the mosque to regain the top of Rue Jemaa ez Zitouna and the **restaurant** where I suggest you have lunch.

This restaurant draws both market traders and suited civil servants from the Dar el Bey; the food (usually a choice of fish, *tajine* or chicken) is cheap and the ambience characterful. If you want something more upmarket and don't mind the company of tour groups, head back down Souk el Attarine to Souk el Trouk (Souk of the Turks). About halfway along its shadowy length a doorway on the right leads up to **Mrabet**, a restaurant built over the tombs of three holy men. A traditional café occupies the ground floor and the restaurant is up the stairs at the rear.

Aim to leave the medina before 2pm, in order to leave a good two hours for the **Bardo Museum** (Tues–Sun winter 9.30am–4.30pm, summer 9am–5pm, closed Mon and feast days). To reach the museum, take a No 3 bus from Avenue Habib Bourguiba, which will drop you outside, or take the No 4 tram (called Métro) from Barcelone Station, Avenue de Paris or Place de la République, and alight at Bardo, from where a short walk leads to the museum (*see map, pages 18–19*).

Perfume-maker, Souk el Attarine

The Bardo occupies a 19th-century palace. It is a curious blend of traditional Moorish architecture, with slender columns, arcaded courtyards and faience tiling, and European classicism. It contains a good Islamic museum (upstairs) but the star exhibits are the Roman mosaics, covering whole walls and floors.

A number of the rooms are devoted to particular towns – for example, the Bulla Regia room (Salle VI, ground floor), the Thuburbo Majus room (Salle IX, ground floor), and the Dougga room (Salle XII, upstairs). Other exhibits are grouped thematically – for example *stelae* and tombs (downstairs corridor leading to the WC), Early Christian finds from Jerba and Tabarka (Salle V, downstairs) and mosaics relating to wild animals (Salle XVI, at the top of the stairs). It is difficult to choose highlights, but don't miss the mosaic of Neptune and the Four Seasons (Salle XII) the mosaic of Virgil attended by the Muses (Virgilus room, first floor) or the one of Ulysses resisting the call of the

Ulysses and the Sirens

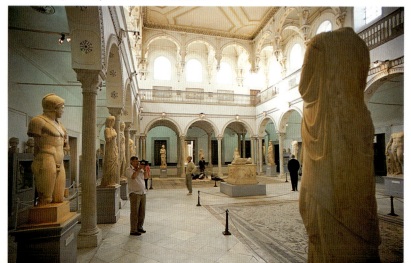

Sirens (Salle XIV). Many of the mosaics depict myths, but others record everyday life in Roman Africa. The agricultural calendar and hunting scenes paint a vivid picture of the region's dual role as the empire's bread-basket and supplier of wild animals for the amphitheatres. The emperors used Roman Africa to settle army veterans, giving them rich agricultural estates in return for their military services, and it was the sumptuous villas of these veterans which contained most of these mosaics. The Bardo closes at 4.30pm, but the pleasantly relaxing gardens are open longer.

Evenings in Tunis are not exactly buzzing. After the burst of early-evening shopping has subsided (by about 7pm) people gravitate to the streets radiating from Avenue Habib Bourguiba. If you are in town from October to June, check upcoming performances at the **theatre** (intersection of Avenue Habib Bourguiba and Rue de Grèce) and in the nightclubs of the main hotels (Hotel Africa El Mouradi and the Oriental Palace Hotel), where a big-name Arab *chanteuse* may be performing (worth seeing not just for the music – usually love songs immortalised by long-dead Egyptians – but also to witness the sheer joy of the audience).

Alternatively just settle for a drink (try the upstairs terrace of the faded but still elegant **Hotel Majestic** on Avenue de Paris) followed by dinner (see *Eating Out* for suggestions) or follow the flashy cars out to the restaurants and nightclubs on the coast between **La Goulette** (good for fish restaurants) and La Marsa. Those without their own transport could hop on the TGM to **Sidi Bou Saïd** for supper followed by jasmine-scented night strolls and a *café Turc* in the perennially popular **Café des Nattes** (see *itinerary 2*).

The Bardo, famous for its Roman mosaics

A day covering the best of ancient Carthage (map overleaf) followed by an evening in the cliff-top village of Sidi Bou Saïd.

Take the TGM (light railway) to Salammbo from the station at the foot of Avenue Habib Bourguiba in Tunis. Wear comfortable shoes and a sunhat; take a swimsuit for bathing. Entrance tickets can be bought at any of the seven sites that comprise ancient Carthage.

The ruins of Ancient Carthage, the great maritime city founded in 814BC, are scattered along the coast to the northeast of Tunis. They lie across the Lake of Tunis, an unprepossessing expanse of water bordered by docks and factories but from late summer made lovelier by visiting flamingos. The strip from La Goulette to La Marsa, including Carthage, is a wealthy residiential area, and flower-clad modern villas ramble over the ancient remains. Ex-President Habib Bourguiba once vowed that if ever Tunisia struck oil on a large scale he would have the money to order the villas' demolition and excavate Carthage properly.

Almost every guidebook stresses how disappointing Carthage is, but providing you prepare for the suburban setting and don't raise your expectations too

The open-air sanctuary of Tophet

high, a day spent touring the dispersed sites can be very satisfying. A brief history of Carthage and the Carthaginians is given in the history section of this book. Officially the sites are open 8am–7pm in summer and 8.30am–5.30pm in winter, closed Sun, though to be on the safe side it is best not to arrive before 8.30am and 9am respectively.

The first of Carthage's sites as you approach from Tunis is the **Tophet** (*Sanctuaire Punique*), the open-air sanctuary where Carthaginian children were sacrificed to the gods Tanit and Baal Hammoum. (Get off the TGM at Carthage Salammbo station, cross the road – do not cross the railway line – and proceed straight ahead; at the stop sign bear left, following signs for *Sanctuaire*

Mask of sacrifice

Punique and passing Résidence de Carthage en route.)

As you enter the Tophet, turn right behind the ticket office and follow the path round. Among the weeds and rubble are scores of *stelae*, some bearing the symbol of the goddess Tanit and one or two the image of a priest carrying a child. The path leads to an underground chamber where the sacrifices took place. The urns containing the charred remains were buried underneath the *stelae*, often accompanied by amulets, beads and grimacing clay masks.

Child sacrifice was practised in Carthage from the time of the city's founding (814BC) until its fall to the Romans in 146BC, though only in times of national crisis. The victims were generally first-born infants up to the age of three; they were strangled first, then placed in the arms of the statue, the flames licking up from below. Afterwards their ashes were placed in urns with prayers of consecration.

Leaving the Tophet, turn right and go down Rue Hannibal towards the **Punic Ports**. There are two ports: the commercial port (so far not restored), which you pass on your right, and the military port, which comes into view straight ahead. Turn right around the edge of the military port and proceed through an avenue of oleander (again you may have to offer a tip if you don't have a ticket). To appreciate the ingenuity of these ports, which may seem disappointing in view of the fame of Carthage as a maritime power, take a look at the displays inside the interesting **Oceanographic Museum** (Tues–Sat

2.30– 5.30pm, sun 10am–noon, separate admission feee) situated between the two ports. Scale models show how the ports would have looked both under the Carthaginians and the Romans. Originally the ports were linked to one another by a channel and had a common entrance, 21m (70ft) wide, from the sea. The military port had an island in its centre, and quays containing shipyards were set at intervals round both the island and the perimeter of the port, affording a capacity for 220 vessels. The whole structure was contained by walls so that the dockyard was concealed from enemy vessels at sea. Remains of one of the dry docks is marked by four piles of stone blocks representing the Ionic columns that once separated the berths.

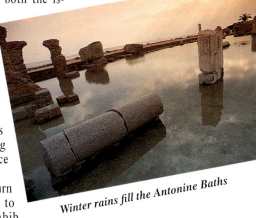

Winter rains fill the Antonine Baths

Out of the Punic Ports, turn right and carry straight on to the main road (Avenue Habib Bourguiba), and turn right again. Proceed along Avenue Bourguiba (a longish but mercifully shady walk) towards the rest of Carthage's sites (if you can't face a walk in the heat you could hop on the TGM and alight at Carthage Hannibal). On the left along the way is the **Paleo-Christian Museum**, containing mainly 5th to 7th-century finds from Roman Carthage, including a lovely statue of Ganymede with his lover Zeus disguised as an eagle.

After the museum the road passes cafés, a supermarket and fruit stalls where you can buy provisions for a picnic lunch. If you would prefer lunch in a restaurant, **Le Neptune**, to the right a little further down the main road, offers a good medium-priced fish and seafood menu and views over the bay. Next door is the **Quartier de Magon** with pavements showing the Punic influence on Roman mosaics.

Follow the seashore to the Antonine baths, which are on the left, but before venturing through the entrance you may like to take a swim off the rocks. The classical backdrop of the ruins and the blissful peace of the spot endow a resonance lacking elsewhere in this suburban setting A swim and a picnic lunch are the perfect prelude to a hot afternoon of ruin-roaming.

The **Antonine Baths** (Thremes d'Antonin) belong to Roman Carthage. The complex is huge, reputedly the largest outside Rome. Through the gates, follow the broad path straight ahead and turn right to a viewing platform and a scale model of the baths. A map carved into a slab of white marble delineates the different parts of the baths. A tall standing pillar gives an idea of the original height of the buildings (the chambers that you see are only the cellars). The Presidential Palace overlooks the baths, so be careful when taking photographs. Taking pictures of the palace is strictly forbidden, and you may have your film confiscated by guards if you point your camera in the wrong direction.

After the baths, visit the **museum** (Musée de Carthage) which, along with the cathedral (now used as a cultural centre), crowns the Hill of Byrsa, claimed to be the original settlement of Queen Dido, the founder of Carthage (see *History and Culture*).To reach the museum from the baths, proceed back up to Avenue 7 Novembre. After passing the entrances to the Roman Villas and the theatre (still in use and worth seeing) look out for a flight of steps on the lef. Climbing these, you reach Rue Jamon. Follow this round and turn left at the end. At the next junction go right and then sharp left up Rue Mendez France. Another flight of steps on the right cuts up to the cathedral.

At the top of the steps a green sign points right to the entrance of the museum (200m/660ft), beyond a courtyard scattered with ancient remains.

Come in to Sidi Bou

The star attractions on the ground floor of the museum are the Punic sarcophagi (the miniature ones were for ashes), in particular a pair of large sarcophagi (4th century BC) of a priest and priestess. The layout and presentation of the upper floor are excellent. Using colour coding, the main room plots the major periods of Carthage: Punic (beige), Roman (blue), Christian (pink) and Arab (green). Each section shows the arts, crafts, weapons and tools of the period. Presenting a micro-chronology of Carthage are two cases of lamps – symbolising illumination and spanning 15 centuries of occupation. At the entrance to the second room (the *Salle Punique*) is a large funeral mask recovered from the Tophet at Salammbo. Also here is a cross-section model of the Tophet with explanatory notes.

Leaving the museum, retrace your steps to the foot of Rue Mendez France and turn right, heading downhill towards the railway line and the sea. At Carthage Hannibal Station, cross to the opposite platform and catch the next TGM to Sidi Bou Saïd.

Affectionately referred to as 'Sidi Bou' by locals, **Sidi Bou Saïd** is a Tunisian village of unrivalled style. Its cobbled streets are flanked by white cube houses with heavy studded doors and blue *mashrabiya* balconies. André Gide described Sidi Bou as 'bathing in a fluid, mother-of-pearl sedative'.

To reach the heart of the village, go with the flow of people. Turn right as you leave the station and head up the hill. At the roundabout bear left and carry on climbing (a one-way system requires cars to branch right just after the roundabout), crossing into the main drag, a steep cobblestoned street strung with souvenirs. Take a right just before this thoroughfare to reach the Moorish palace of the Baron Rodolphe d'Erlanger (1872–1932), now the **Centre des Musiques Arabes et Mediterranéennes** (Tues–Sun, winter 9am–1pm and 2–5pm, summer 9am– 12.30pm and 3–6.30pm; admission fee), displaying a collection of musical instruments.

Afterwards return to the main street. A short way up on the left is **Dar el Annabi** (Tues–Sun 9am–7.30pm; admission fee), a traditional middle-class house, with authentic decor, several tableaux and a beautiful courtyard, which provides a delightful glimpse of Tunisian life. The family still lives in the house, and serves mint tea to visitors in the inner courtyard.

Continue up the main street to the **Café des Nattes**, where the capital's young and trendy like to hang out. Bear right and follow the road to just past the restaurant Ayyam Zaman (Au Bon Vieux Temps) where a small road forks right to **Café Sidi Chabanne**. This cliff-top café enjoys one of the best locations in Tunisia. Squeeze on to a bench (the café is packed on summer evenings), order a *thé au pignons* (mint laced tea with pine kernels) and buy a posy of jasmine. Back towards Café des Nattes are three restaurants with al fresco dining:

Sidi Bou, a Tunisian village of unrivalled style

the excellent but expensive **Ayyam Zaman**, the pleasant **Dar Zarrouk** and the cheaper **Charguis**.

After dinner retire to Café des Nattes, to sit cross-legged on the dais and sip *café Turc*. The train service from La Marsa back to Tunis, which stops at Sidi Bou Saïd, runs until around midnight (check exact times at the station).

3. Cap Bon

A day exploring Cap Bon: hot springs, fine beaches, a fish lunch and the Punic site of Kerkouane. See map on p. 35.

A car is essential for this trip. Although designed as a day's outing from Tunis, this circular tour is also a good option for anyone based in Hammamet. It includes several specific attractions, but much of the appeal of Cap Bon lies in the quiet, rural scenery and gentle flow of life. Take a bathing costume.

Though within hazy view of the capital, Cap Bon is far from Tunis in terms of its development. Parts of the peninsula have only recently received electricity.

Miraculously, in spite of the silky white sands that line both coasts only Hammamet and Nabeul at the foot of the cape have been developed for tourism. Cereals, vegetables and fruit are the main source of income, especially tomatoes, citrus fruits and vines; if you are here in September, look out for the wine festival in Grombalia.

Leave Tunis by the GP No 1 (to Hammam Lif). At Borj Cedria, turn off to Soliman (the signpost is smack-bang on the turning, so be careful not to overshoot it) and follow the road to **Korbous**, a health spa since Roman times, when it was Aquae Calidau Carpitanae. Springs (both hot and cold) abound in this area. Leaving the grim-looking hotel-clinics (Ain Oktor Hotel and Hôtel les Sources) to the seriously afflicted, make your way to **Ait Atrous** (signalled by a clutch of cafés and grill restaurants), which offers a less formal way of sampling the waters a few hundred metres past the village, just before the road climbs away from the

El Haouaria, famous for falconry

coast. Below the cafés, a scalding hot spring gushes out of the bank and tips into the sea in a cloud of sulphurous steam. Join bathers in the invigorating waters (both men and women are welcome but swimming costumes must be worn). Afterwards relax over a coffee on the terrace of the roadside café.

Beyond Korbous the road climbs steeply and meanders inland through plume-topped cane, olive groves, gum and cypress trees, and vineyards. Turn sharp left at the Brir Mroua junction, following the road to El Haouaria. If you fancy an hour or so on the fine white sands of **Plage Rtiba** (wonderful bathing in crystal-clear waters) look out for a makeshift sign. The 2km (1¼ mile)-track is easy-going, but don't attempt to drive on to the sands: out of season there may not be anyone around to help haul you out. In the summer, rush huts are hired out to campers.

El Haouaria, at the tip of Cap Bon, is famous for falconry.

Mohammed

Young peregrine falcons and sparrowhawks are caught on their spring migration and trained for a special falconry festival held in June. Afterwards most of the birds are set free to resume their inter-continental flight. Unless you happen to be here during the festival, when you may want to join in the fun, drive through the village and head for the peninsula's tip and the town's other claim to fame, the **ancient quarries** (*Grottes Romaines*) (daily, winter 8.30am–5.30pm, summer 8am–7pm; admission fee), passing on your way the Restaurant Les Grottes, a good option for lunch on your return. A new road runs down to the caves. Before joining the local *guide des Grottes*, for a tour, have a beer on the terrace of the adjoining café (eschew the food – it's quite expensive and not that good) and admire the view. The small island offshore is Zembra.

The caves (tip the guide) have been quarried since Carthaginian times. From this point, the limestone blocks could be easily and quickly loaded on to barges bound for Carthage. Archaeologists have found Cap Bon tombs of El Haouaria limestone dating from the 6th century BC.

After lunch, follow the coast road round to **Kerkouane** (Tuesday

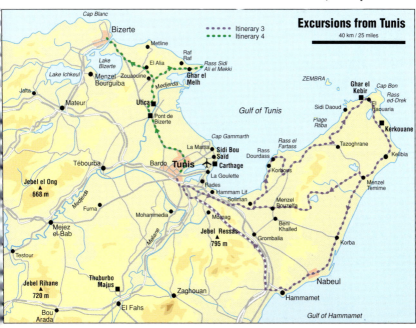

to Sunday, winter 8.30am–5.30pm, summer 8am–7pm; admission fee), a Punic settlement perched on the edge of the sea and perfumed by wild herbs. Unlike other Punic sites, Kerkouane was not rebuilt by the Romans or the Arabs and therefore offered a clear picture of Carthaginian life to the archaeologists who discovered it in 1952.

The settlement was a base for the manufacture of Tyrian Purple, a dye derived from the shellfish murex, but finds (see the museum adjoining the site) indicate that the town also supported a thriving community of craftsmen. Particularly striking is the town's plumbing: well-appointed bathrooms, complete with hip-baths lined with red cement. Look out for the sign of the goddess Tanit (a triangle with a head and two arms) in white marble chips on a floor.

Some 10km (6 miles) south of the turning to Kerkouane lies **Kelibia**, which supports a little low-key tourism, and has a handsome Byzantine fortress (daily winter 8.30am–5.30pm, summer 8am–7pm; admission fee). After climbing up to the fort, drive down to the fishing harbour, where the popular café **Sidi el-Bahri** on the western edge, offers a peaceful stop with mint tea and waterpipes.

Carry on to Menzel Temime. From here you have a choice: cut back to Tunis via Menzel Bouzelfa, a pretty ride through scented orange groves, or continue down the coast to Hammamet, a good option for those who don't mind a late drive back.

Since its development from a small fishing village in the 1960s, **Hammamet** has grown long tentacles of hotels radiating from a nucleus of restaurants, crêperies and ice-cream parlours. Though the kasbah is now a warren of souvenir shops, it is not without attraction, in particular the **Café Sidi Bou Hadid**, tucked into a corner of the walls. To find this stylish café, follow the kasbah's main drag of souvenir shops to the end

Passing time in Hammamet

and turn right down a short alley, which emerges in the café's courtyard. Take a mat-covered pew, order tea and submit to the hypnotic strains of taped *mahlouf* (Tunisian trance music) or *rai*, more upbeat and the favoured background music of the waiters.

For dinner, I recommend either **Restaurant de la Poste**, near the taxi station opposite the medina, or the excellent fish restaurant **Chez Achour**, with a terrace, on Rue Ali Belahouane.

From Hammamet the drive back to Tunis (63km/39 miles) along the autoroute is straightforward and fast (leave the centre of Hammamet via Avenue du Kuwait and take the southern beach road out of town).

Kasbah and beach, Hammamet

Utica was a base in the Roman Civil War

4. North to Bizerte

The Roman ruins at Utica, the old pirate lair of Ghar el Melh and the beach at Rass Sidi Ali el Mekhi. Overnight stay at the Petit Mousse in Bizerte (Tel: 72-432185 to book well ahead). A car is essential. Pack your swimming costume. See map on p. 35.

This trip is not designed as a circular tour, but if you prefer to go back to Tunis rather than stay in Bizerte there shouldn't be any problem covering the return distance in one day. Leave Tunis from Boulevard du 20 Mars 1956, which radiates from Bab Saadoun north of the medina. See map on page 35.

The peaceful countenance of the coastal region to the north of Tunis belies its long and eventful history at the cutting edge of Tunisian involvement with Europe: the Roman town of Utica sided with Rome rather than Carthage in the Punic Wars and was Pompey's North African base in the Roman Civil War; Ghar el Melh, lying on a concealed lagoon just north of Utica, was a lair of Barbary coast pirates between the 16th and 18th centuries, and Bizerte was a key base for Axis powers (and a target for Allied bombs) during World War II.

This corner of Tunisia is practically untouched by package tourism; so far only the Tunisians themselves and a handful of French are familiar with its first-rate beaches, the excellent Petit Mousse restaurant/hotel in Bizerte, and Lake Ichkeul, a World Heritage wetland site.

The hoardings and high-rises that line the P8 from Tunis peter out at **Pont de Bizerte** (25km/15 miles) and the scenery settles into rural patterns, with agricultural workers busy in the fields and children selling produce to passing cars. About 5km (3 miles) beyond here, look out for the sign *Utique Ruine*, pointing right to the Roman town of **Utica**. The site (Tues–Sun, winter 8.30am–5.30pm, summer 8am–7pm; admission fee) lies some 2km (1 mile) down the lane, beyond the attendant museum. As a result, it is not unusual to have this peaceful spot all to yourself.

Before the Mejerda river silted up, Utica was on the sea. According to Pliny the Elder, it was founded as a way-station by Phoenician sailors from Tyre in about 1101BC, some 300 years before Carthage. It gained a reputation for treachery: Agothocles of Syracuse used it as a base from which to attack Carthage in 310BC, and in 146BC it was the Roman general Scipio's base in the Third (and final) Punic War. In return for supporting Rome, Utica was briefly capital of Roman Africa.

Make your way to the **Maison de la Cascade** (marked by a cluster of cypress trees), the most interesting of the villas. This large and obviously luxurious house (AD69–96) takes its name from the pool gracing its central courtyard. Off to the side of the courtyard, notice the *triclinium* (dining-room), distinguished by its handsome marble floor; the plain U-shaped border would have been covered by banquettes, obviating the need for any decoration. The house has a set of fish-theme mosaics *in situ* – lift the wooden lids to view. As you leave the house by the front door (note the notches which would have contained the roof beams), you face the Punic necropolis, the source of many of the grave goods in the museum (same opening hours as the site) back up the road.

The old port of Bizerte

When you leave Utica, instead of returning to the main Tunis-Bizerte road, carry on along the lane to **Ghar el Melh** (Cave of Salt) on the peninsula's tip, turning left at the mosque with a silver dome and right at the following two junctions (both signposted). The one-time pirate lair of Ghar el Melh (formerly known as Porto Farina) lies sandwiched between the hilly ridge of Jebel Nadour and a slumbrous lagoon, the perfect slip for the shallow-draughted vessels of the corsairs.

The road through Ghar el Melh proceeds along the densely-

farmed edge of the lagoon, from where a left track leads to **Rass Sidi Ali el Mekhi**, a beach of soft white sands cradled by green headland. The tomb of Sidi Ali el Mekhi draws a thin trickle of old ladies on donkeys. If you fancy a picnic on the beach, buy provisions before leaving Ghar el Melh (the market is off the road tunnel in the village centre); alternatively, there are a couple of basic restaurants. The 3-km (2-mile) track to the beach is an easy drive, but muddy out of season.

From Ghar el Melh head for Bizerte via El Alia (turning just before Zouaouine).

Bizerte, a fledgling resort and an important port, underwent rapid development under the French, who wanted to counteract the strength of British bases in Gibraltar and Malta. Jules Ferry, the father of French colonialism, said: 'If I have taken Tunisia, it is to have Bizerte!' The Italians described the town as 'a pistol levelled at the heart of Italy'. It was the last piece of Tunisia to be surrendered by the French.

If you intend to stay the night as I recommend, I suggest you first check in to Le Petit Mousse, overlooking the ocean on the Route de la Corniche on the north side of town, and then drive back to explore the *centre ville*. The chief attraction of Bizerte for the tourist is the picturesque old port, off to the left at the foot of Avenue Habib Bourguiba, with its peeling colonial-cum-Moorish architecture, painted fishing boats and sheltering kasbah. Also of interest are the Spanish Fort and the medina.

After taking tea on the quay, head up Avenue Habib Bourguiba and follow the sign to the **Monument of the Martyrs** (not to be confused with the Place des Martyrs near the old casino). This gigantic concrete arch rising over a sea of headstones commemorates the Bizerte Crisis of 1961, when 1,365 Tunisians were killed by French troops following escalating disturbances over continued French presence in the town.

The evening is best spent over a meal on the terrace of Le Petit Mousse, cracking open a bottle of Château Mornag and listening to the surf breaking on the beach. The high standards of this small hotel and restaurant are rare in Tunisia, so I suggest that you splash out and dine in style (prices are very reasonable). Next morning either head back to Tunis, or set off for the northwest of Tunisia – the region featured in the next section of this guide – via the lovely Lake Ichkeul (daily 7am–7pm), a haven for wintering and migrating birds.

The Northwest

The Khroumiria, the region bordering Algeria north of the Mejerda river, is dramatically different from the rest of Tunisia. At the tail end of the Atlas Mountains, a range that rises in Morocco, the Khroumiria is wooded and hilly, attracting hunters in winter and hikers in summer, when the altitude renders temperatures attractively cool. Before the French protectorate the Khroumiria's Berbers were renowned for their fierce independence and disregard for the law. Their cattle-rustling raids into Algeria gave the French a pretext for invading Tunisia in 1881.

A fertile region

At the coast, the Khroumiria drops to Tabarka, a quiet seaside town with a few low-key hotels, a plethora of shops selling coral jewellery, a magnificent swathe of dune-backed sand and a Genoese fort basking on an island offshore. If you want to spend a few days relaxing on a beach, scuba diving or snorkelling and eating freshly caught fish at inexpensive prices, Tabarka is the ideal base.

On the south side of the Khroumiria, the land subsides to Jendouba and the high wheat-growing plateau of the Tell. It was here that the Romans built Bulla Regia with its sumptuous underground villas, a mode of building unique in the Roman world.

The Northwest

40 km / 25 miles

● ● ● ● Itinerary 5
● ● ● ● Itinerary 6

Cap Serrat
Cap Negro
Sejenane
Cap Roux
Tabarka
Start
J. Guessa
805 m
TUNISIA
Nefza
El Kala
Lake Oubeïra
Lake Tonga
Babouch
ALGERIA
Ain Draham
Béja
Hammam Bourguiba
Fernana
J. bou Khrezara
877 m
Bulla Regia
Bou Salem
Thibar
Médjerda
Jendouba
Téboursouk
Ghardimaou
Dougga
Souk Jamaa
Musti
Touiret
Sidi Merzoug
El Krib
Gaâfour
O. Mellegue
Sakiet Sidi Youssef
El Kef
Start
Henchir Lorbeuss
Siliana
Cap Serrat

5. The Khroumiria

A leisurely morning in the seaside resort of Tabarka, followed by a seafood lunch and an afternoon drive through the Khroumiria mountains to the Roman site of Bulla Regia. A car is essential. Pack a bathing costume for the morning in Tabarka.

This itinerary is designed as a linear trip taking you through three very different landscapes. Accommodation can be found in Tabarka, Ain Draham and Jendouba (see Practical Information) but if you are including this route as part of a wider motoring tour, I recommend that you drive on to El Kef, the starting point of Itinerary 6. El Kef's Hotel Les Pins (Tel: 78-204300) is modest but with comfortable rooms and lovely views over the valley.

The wealth of early Christian mosaics from Thrabaca, the Roman forerunner of **Tabarka**, have been transplanted to a special room in the Bardo Museum in Tunis, so sights in the town are few, but it is easy enough to while away a morning; once you have explored the fort, taken a dip and priced the coral jewellery in the shops on Avenue Habib Bourguiba, it will be time for lunch.

Begin when temperatures are still reasonably cool with a walk up to the **Genoese Fort**. A causeway now connects the island with the mainland, but the easiest way to get to the top is to cross the small beach and scramble up one of the paths (they join the broad road leading to the fort's entrance). A notice in Arabic forbids entry (the fort belongs to the Ministry of Defence), but anyone I have ever encountered up here – usually the keeper of the lighthouse that occupies a section of the fort – has encouraged me to wander round providing I don't take photographs.

This island was acquired by the Lomellini and Grimaldi families in 1542, when it was traded for Draghut, the 'drawn sword of Islam', a corsair captured by a Genoese galley some years before. The Genoese wanted the island on account of the highly lucrative coral

Tabarka's Genoese Fort

The theatre at Bulla Regia

reefs that lie off these shores. In spite of the proximity of the Muslim mainland, a community of some 1,200 Christians held the island until 1741, when they were expelled by Ali Pasha.

The peace and pine-scented breezes are soothing. If you fancy a cooling swim and an hour or so lying in the sun, clamber down the hill on the far side of the fort, where you will find good bathing off the rocks (beware urchins), or rejoin the beach and walk through the surf towards the new hotel developments across the bay. On your way back to town, follow the shore round to the right to see Les Aiguilles, a pack of needle-shaped stacks.

Tabarka's main street is Avenue Habib Bourguiba, which runs to the harbour. The ex-president Bourguiba was, as a young nationalist, placed under house arrest in Tabarka's Hôtel de France. Coral shops dominate the street and its side alleys. Their keepers exert surprisingly slight pressure on potential customers and it is possible to browse at leisure. Asking prices begin at around £50 for a simple bracelet to £500 for a multi-stranded cut and polished necklace. If you are serious about buying, bargain hard.

Ready for lunch? Claim a table on the terrace of the restaurant of **Hotel les Aiguilles** (corner of avenues Habib Bourguiba and Hedi Chaker) which has a very reasonable menu of fish and Tunisian specialities.

Lunch at Montazah

Afterwards set off for **Aïn Draham** (Spring of Money), along the Babouch/Aïn Draham road (signposted). The road runs straight as a die for the first 12km (7 miles), then spirals into the hills, nudging the Algerian border at Babouch. Watch out for kamikaze vendors of wooden bowls, ornamental hatstands and pine nuts/walnuts/strawberries (depending on season). At Aïn Draham, the heart of the Khroumiria, stop off at **Hôtel Beau Séjour**, an ivy-clad hunting lodge, for coffee and fresh air on the terrace.

Past Fernana the sylvan scenery yields to the wheatland of the Tell. **Bulla Regia** (daily, winter 8.30am–5.30pm, summer 8am–7pm; admission fee) is signposted off to the left about 10km (6 miles) before Jendouba. After a few more kilometres the site comes into view on the left-hand side of the lane.

Entering the site, proceed straight ahead, between the walls of two buildings. At the yellow signposts turn right. The entrance to the **baths of Julia Memnia** (3rd century AD), named after the wife of the Libyan-born Emperor Septimius Severus, are now on your right. As you step down into the complex, examine the vaulting where remnants of clay piping, an architectural device used to fashion vaulted ceilings and arches, can still be seen. Continuing along the main street beside the baths, you come to the **Bibliothèque** (library), complete with moat, and then the **Temple of Isis** (both on the right). The main route continues to a gem of a **theatre**, complete with a bear mosaic (restored).

Leaving the theatre, retrace your steps for a few metres and then take the route branching up towards the hillside behind the site. You will pass the market on the left and emerge at the forum with the Temple of Apollo up ahead and the basilica on your right. Bearing left past the capitol, continue until you come to another right-turn towards the hills. This leads to Bulla Regia's most remarkable remains, the **underground villas**.

Why Bulla Regia's inhabitants built underground can only be surmised. Respite from the heat is the most logical explanation, though hotter places in the Roman empire did not follow suit. One of the most splendid villas is the **Maison de la Chasse** (House of the Hunt), situated next to a small mound on the right-hand side of the path. Note the well and the remains of an oil press inside the entrance. The flight of steps leading to the underground chambers emerges in a colonnaded atrium that is handsomely decorated with geometric mosaics.

Regain the main street and continue to the top. Here, turn right and at the next junction follow the yellow sign to the **Maison de la Pêche** (House of the Fish), notable for its fish mosaics *in situ*. Afterwards proceed to the **Maison d'Amphitrite** (signposted from the junction), which contains the lovely Triumph of Venus, a mosaic depicting Venus borne by Tri-

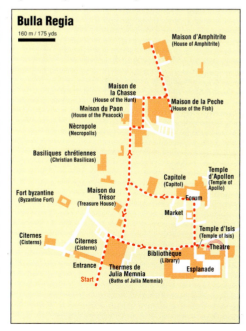

Bulla Regia

160 m / 175 yds

Maison d'Amphitrite
(House of Amphitrite)

Maison de
la Chasse
(House of the Hunt)

Maison de la Peche
(House of the Fish)

Maison du Paon
(House of the Peacock)

Nècropole
(Necropolis)

Basiliques chrétiennes
(Christian Basilicas)

Capitole
(Capitol)

Temple
d'Apollon
(Temple of
Apollo)

Fort byzantine
(Byzantine Fort)

Maison du
Trèsor
(Treasure House)

Forum

Market

Citernes
(Cisterns)

Citernes
(Cisterns)

Temple d'Isis
(Temple of Isis)

Theatre

Bibliothèque
(Library)

Entrance

Thermes de
Julia Memnia
(Baths of Julia Memnia)

Esplanade

Start

tons and attended by Amor, astride a dolphin, carrying her crown, mirror and jewel box.

On your return from the House of Amphitrite, stop at the **Maison de la Nouvelle Chasse** (House of the New Hunt), behind the Maison de la Chasse. A fragmentary mosaic on the ground floor depicts hunting scenes: hunting horns, servants carrying a python, a figure on a horse, a tiger consuming an antelope. The Empire's amphitheatres were stocked with wild animals captured in the Khroumiria and shipped back to Rome from Tabarka. The last lion was reputedly shot in the region in the 1830s and the last panther in 1932.

Before leaving Bulla Regia, take a look inside the museum (next to the car park), which includes finds from Punic Bulla Regia.

To reach El Kef (Le Kef), a further 62km (39 miles), drive into Jendouba and turn right at the roundabout marked by the top of a Corinthian column. The route wends through undulating hills planted with wheat – a vivid reminder that this region was once the bread-basket of the Roman Empire.

6. Ancient Towns of the Tell

A full day beginning at El Kef and proceeding to the spectacular Roman ruins of Dougga (68km/42 miles). Staying overnight in the 2-star Hotel Thugga in Teboursouk. See map on p. 40.

Buses run hourly from El Kef to Teboursouk and it is easy enough to hitch the 6-km (4-mile) ride to Dougga from there.

Stacked into a spur of the Jebel Dyr, **El Kef** (the rock) enjoys a commanding location, which along with its status as the capital of the northern border region raises it above other towns of the Tell. It has an ancient history, first entering chronicles as the Carthaginian town of Sicca. Following defeat in the First Punic War it was overrun by battalions of disaffected mercenaries, who eventually rebelled in a savage battle known as the Truceless War. Under the Romans, Sicca became Sicca Veneria (the name of one of the town's hotels), a suffix alluding to the salacious rites of Venus which went on in the town's temples.

In view of what is in store later in the day, leave El Kef's scanty Roman remains to the enthusiasts and concentrate on its Arab heritage, in particular on Sidi Bou Makhlouf Mosque and the kasbah. To find the mosque, climb the steps next to the Hôtel des Sources, diagonally opposite Hotel Sicca Veneria in the town centre, and turn right at the top, following the sign.

With its dragooned domes, octagonal minaret and whitewashed walls, the **Sidi**

Berber country

Sidi Bou Makhlouf Mosque

Bou Makhlouf Mosque is one of the most attractive in Tunisia. It is the focal point of the medina; men congregate in the shade of its walls to chat and listen to the recitations drifting through its doors. Fourteenth-century, it is nowhere near as old as the **Old Mosque**, pristinely restored next door. This austere stone building functioned as a mosque from the 8th century but dates from the 4th century, when it was probably a Christian church.

To reach the **kasbah** (admission fee) climb up the bank behind Sidi Bou Makhlouf Mosque, from where a broad path leads up to the gates. It's worth coming up for the views over the plain and the cool breezes blowing through the battlements. Nearby on the Place Sidi Ali Aïssa, the **Museum of Popular Arts and Traditions** (Tues–Sun, winter 9.30am–4.30pm, summer 9am–1pm and 4–7pm; admission fee) has interesting displays on Tunisia's nomads and their way of life.

Back on Avenue Habib Bourguiba, pick up provisions for a picnic (try a sandwich: a *baton* of French bread crammed with chicken or *merguez*, salad, olives and chips) and set off on the road for Dougga (follow signs for Teboursouk/Tunis), a pleasant ride through changing scenery of rolling wheatfields, olive groves and cactus. El Krib is the only place of any size en route. Just past here look out for the ruins of Musti scattered either side of the road, in particular a bereft arch on the right.

Ancient **Dougga** (Thugga) (Tues–Sun, winter 8.30am–5.30pm, summer 8am–7pm; admission fee) appears in the hills on the left as you pass the modern village of Dougga. The easiest access, however, is via Teboursouk (look out for the sharp left-hand turn as you drive up towards Teboursouk from the main El Kef-Tunis road; a 4-km/2-mile lane loops round behind the ridge). The extensive site

Dougga's Capitolene Temple

is well labelled and signposted, and an excellent official guide is on hand. However, the setting is so magnificent that it is tempting simply to wander.

Dougga was already established when the Romans arrived in the 2nd century AD. In the 2nd century BC it was the base of Massinissa, a local chieftain who, to his enduring advantage, supported Rome against Carthage.

First stop is the back row of the heavily restored 2nd-century **theatre** (first building on the right as you enter the site), a good spot to unpack your picnic and survey the ruins spread out below. Built into the side of the hill, it commands panoramic views over the pink and mauve plain. It was designed for an audience of 3,500, and still draws a good crowd for the Festival of Drama in the summer.

Out of the theatre turn right and walk along the paved street leading to the Plaza of the Winds, the Capitolene Temple and the Forum, passing the small Temple of Augustan Piety on your left and later the Temple of Mercury on your right. Following the route round to the Forum, step down into the **Plaza of the Winds**, and look for a circular carving in the paving, a compass recording the names of the 12 winds.

Next to the square is the lofty **Capitolene Temple**, faced by four Corinthian pillars and still bearing in its pediment a crumbling carving of the Emperor Antonius Pius entwined with an eagle – perhaps being taken to join the immortals. It is dedicated to Jupiter, Juno and Minerva and to the glory of co-emperors Marcus Aurelius and Lucus Verus. Inside, look out for three niches, designed to contain statues of the gods, and a severed head of Jupiter.

From the Capitolene Temple proceed slightly left, then straight ahead and down some steps to the **Temple of Tellus**, dedicated to the goddess of the earth and the protector of marriage, fertility and the dead (some villas with mosaic flooring still intact) and a building called **Dar el Acheb** (House of the Herbalist), though its true purpose is a mystery.

Dougga

160 m / 175 yds

to Teboursouk

Tombes romaines (Roman Tombs)
Temple of Saturn
Dolmens
Temple of Minerva
Tombes romaines (Roman Tombs)
Cistern
Aïn Mizeb (Spring)
Aqueduct
Tombes romaines (Roman Tombs)
Entrance and Car Park
Spring
Amphitheatre
Theatre
Aqueduct d'Aïn El Hammam
Cistern
Arc de Sévère Alexandre (Arch of Alexander Severus)
Tombes romaines (Roman Tombs)
Temple of Mercury
Maison de Fouilles (Excavation House)
Temple of Juno Caelestis
Capitolene Temple
Forum
Plaza of the Winds
Maison des Saisons (House of the Seasons)
Temple Latrines
Baths of Licinius
Tombes romaines (Roman Tombs)
Dar el Acheb (House of the Herbalist)
Maison du Trifolium (House of the Trifolium)
Thermes des Cyclopes (Cyclops Baths)
Cistern
Arc de Septime Sévère (Arch of Septimius Severus)
Baths
Aïn Doura (Spring)
Mausolée Lybico - punique (Punic Mausoleum)

Exiting from Dar el Acheb, turn left and proceed straight ahead, turning left at the top of a small flight of steps and following the signpost to the lovely **Temple of Juno Caelestis**, with its cluster of columns and semi-circular colonnade. Off to the right, behind some olive trees, notice the **Arch of Alexander Severus**, the great-nephew of Septimius Severus (who is commemorated by a Triumph arch on the eastern side of the site). Just above the arch is the **Aqueduct d'Ain El Hammam** which brought water from the spring at El Hammam, some 12km (7 miles) away, a hot source used by local people to this day.

From here, return to the Plaza of the Winds and take the broad paved street to the right of the small mosque (identified by its green door). This way you pass on the left the **Temple of Concordia** and the larger **Temple of Liber Pater** and, down steps on the right, the **Baths of Licinius**, a vast complex of hot and cold rooms, with attendant *palaestra* (gymnasium). Leave the baths via one of the underground passages at the lower level, rejoin the main street (heading downhill) and cut right to the entrance of the **House of the Trifolium** (the brothel), complete with cubicles. Sadly, the stone phallus that once advertised it has gone. Next to the brothel as you descend is the **Cyclops Baths**, with a 12-seater lavatory to the left of the entrance. Still further down is the **Triumphant Arch of Septimius Severus**, the first African emperor.

Dougga's Baths of Licinius

The last call on this tour is the **Punic Mausoleum**, the obelisk at the foot of the site. After its destruction in 1910 by the British consul Thomas Read, who removed its inscription for the British Museum, the four-tier obelisk was restored. Unfortunately the pristine pointing and carving have erased all hint of its 3rd-century BC origins.

Leaving the site, proceed back to the main El Kef to Tunis road and turn left. **Hotel Thugga**, the most comfortable hotel in the region, is a little way along on the left. Rooms are arranged around a courtyard, with rural views to the rear. As **Teboursouk** is quiet even by Tunisian standards, your best bet for the evening is to dine at the hotel (alcohol served), followed by a night-cap of *Boukha* (a fig-based Tunisian firewater) and early bed.

Sousse

A substantial proportion of the 5.4 million tourists that pour into Tunisia annually are bound for the resort of Sousse. Opalescent waters and deep white sands stretch from Port el Kantaoui, a marina-cum-apartment complex 9km (5 miles) north of the city, to Monastir, with its international airport and 18-hole golf course, 20km (12 miles) to the south.

Like Hammamet, the area was developed in the mid-1960s. Within a decade it was bristling with hotels and vying with other Mediterranean hotspots in the bid to win European tourists. Development is continuing, though the mechanical diggers and gaunt cranes have mostly played their role and gardens now engirdle their blindingly-white produce.

Unfortunately, away from the coast and the diversions it offers, the region can seem dull – a vast plain of olive groves and *sebkhet* (salt lagoons). However, there are several interesting sights and towns within easy reach, and I have devised two circular tours linking them. First, though, I include a morning walk round Sousse, a city which, despite its cheery holiday hat (more *ich liebe dich* than kiss-me-quick), has a vibrant local medina, important examples of early Arab architecture and a superb archaeological museum containing finds from Hadrumatum, Sousse's Roman forebear.

Sousse's beach is a major attraction

A morning or afternoon walking the medina, concentrating on the Great Mosque, the Ribat and the archaeological museum.

The focal point of **Sousse** is the walled medina that rises behind the coastal strip. Whatever delights the hotels and beach-clubs devise, it is to the medina that people naturally gravitate when the sun and sand begin to pall.

Begin the morning on Place des Martyrs, next to Place Farhat Hached, the busy square where trains, cars and humans all converge. Enter the **medina** through the breach in its walls (behind the

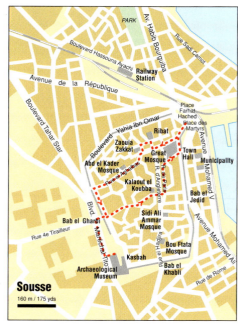

Medina market

port end of the Gardens of Farhat Hached) caused by Allied bombing during World War II. This quickly emerges in front of the buff-coloured **Great Mosque** (8am–2pm, closed Fri; a small entrance allows non-Muslims into the courtyard) and close by, to the right, the **Ribat** (winter 8.30am–5.30pm and summer 8am–7pm, closed Mon; admission fee), with its distinctive *nador* (look-out tower). Both the Great Mosque and the Ribat date from the early years of Arab expansion, hence their militaristic bearing and the extreme depth of their walls – Sousse had no natural defence from attack by land. The Ribat (late 8th century) was one in a chain of fortress-monasteries that encircled the North African coast. It was occupied by *murabatin*, warrior-monks, whose task was to defend the new Muslim faith *be-siff* (by the sword). Inside, climb up to the *nador*, passing the cells where the *murabatin* slept and, at the top of the steps to the upper level, a prayer hall complete with *mihrab* (niche indicating the direction of Mecca). The *nador* affords good views of the port to the fore, over the rooftops to the Khalef el Fela Watchtower of the kasbah behind, and into the courtyard of the 9th-century Great Mosque (also look out for the octagonal green-and-white tiled minaret of the Zaouia Zakkat, your next landmark on this itinerary). The beauty of both the Ribat and the Great Mosque lies in their simplicity, not their ornamentation, in spite of recycled Corinthian columns plundered from Roman sites.

Saving the gauntlet of souvenir stalls for your return through the medina, head up to the kasbah via the **Zaouia Zakkat**, with its highly decorated minaret (to find it, walk past the Ribat Drink Café, following the walls of the Ribat). The *zaouia* was originally an Aghlabid *ribat*, though the three-tiered minaret is Turkish. In front of the Zaouia turn left, then right, immediately left again and then right to join Rue El Aghalba, a quiet thoroughfare that leads to the kasbah's walls.

Turn left at Rue Abou Naouas, keeping the kasbah's walls on your right. At the police station, marked by a flag, strike right through the gate to the main road, Boulevard Maréchal Tito. Two hundred metres (650ft) to the left is the entrance to the **Archaeological Museum** (winter 9am–noon and 2–5.30pm; summer 9am–noon and 3–6pm; closed Mon; admission fee). This superb museum contains mosaics from the Sousse/El Jem region, which are enhanced by the 15th-century kasbah setting.

Medusa mosaic

As you enter, turn right into a courtyard. In the floor, near the threshold, is a 2nd-century mosaic of the Greek Gorgon Medusa, so hideous that anyone who clapped eyes on her was immediately turned to stone. Proceed clockwise round the courtyard for theatrical masks, a handsome bird and beast mosaic, and tile reliefs depicting Adam and Eve and St Theodore (later St George), taken from the walls of Byzantine basilicas (Sousse was a key stronghold of the Byzantines). The room opposite the entrance is covered in large mosaics: Neptune spying on a bacchante being seduced by a satyr (2nd-century); 'the triumph of Bacchus' (Dionysus – here identified as Bacchus – being pulled in a chariot by four tigers and attended by satyrs, a leopard and a lion).

Also off the courtyard is a room dedicated to Carthaginian Sousse, primarily to *stelae* recovered during excavation of the *tophet* (the place of sacrifice). The oldest *stelae* marked the ashes of children, but those of a later date are from animal cremations.

Through the museum's garden of pomegranates and vines is a row of galleries whose mosaics roll over whole walls and floors. The calendar from El Jem, in the first room, displays several rare characteristics. Not only are the seasons depicted in the left-hand column male rather than female, but the figures and scenes representing the months are drawn from religious feast days rather than the more common agricultural cycle. Some of these festivals were particular to Rome, which suggests the mosaic was commissioned by an educated man of Italian descent who wanted to parade his superior social standing. To the left of the calendar is a black and white mosaic incorporating the swastika motif, a common deflector of evil.

The second room contains a magnificent T-shaped *triclinium* (dining-room) floor decoration depicting combat in the amphitheatre (steps lead to a viewing platform). Oddly, the gladiators' quarry are gentle beasts: antelope, ostriches and asses. To the side of this mosaic, concealed in a niche, is a 3rd-century statue of Priapus – painfully mutilated in a later, more prudish, age.

From this side of the museum, climb on to the ramparts for cool breezes and panoramic views over the medina and bay.

Leaving the kasbah, return along Boulevard Maréchal Tito and retrace your steps through the gate. Round the corner to the right of the police station is a café with a terrace, a good spot to prise open a bottle of Boga and recuperate. Afterwards, turn left and head back to the start, branching left at Rue de Paris and emerging on Place des Martyrs at Hotel Medina. Your progress will depend on your resistance to the brass trays, toy camels and leather pouffes that clutter the route.

8. Kairouan, Holy City

A day trip to Kairouan, returning via the Berber village of Takrouna and Port el Kantaoui, Tunisia's showcase resort.

To see all the places recommended in this itinerary, private transport is essential. However, if you don't want to hire a car, it is quick and easy to reach Kairouan by bus or grand-taxi *from Sousse, and taxis and a Noddy train ply the 9km (5 miles) between Sousse and Port el Kantaoui (also known as Sousse-Nord). As this trip involves visiting mosques, wear respectable dress. Car-drivers should leave Sousse via the kasbah.*

A trip to Kairouan, Tunisia's religious heart, is the most popular excursion from the coastal resorts. The city lies a comfortable 57km (35 miles) from Sousse, and promises holy balm (it's the fourth holiest city in Islam and has over 130 mosques) and magic carpets (weaving is a major craft). Cubist Paul Klee claimed Kairouan altered his life: 'Colour has taken hold of

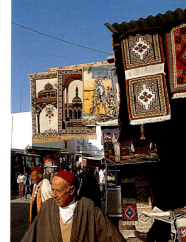

Woven in Kairouan

The medina, Kairouan

me...colour and I are one,' he rhapsodised in his diary.

However, Paul Klee came here in 1914. Today, many are disappointed by Kairouan – at least on first acquaintance. The city stands isolated in a depression on the plain – baking hot in summer and the victim of flash floods in autumn and spring – and spills untidily from its walls. Its 9th-century Great Mosque can seem bleak and utilitarian for a place of worship.

But if you close your eyes to half-finished outskirts (and fellow tourists), and concentrate on the peace of the mosques, the slap of pilgrims' sandals on the *sahns* (courtyards), and the colours of the alleyways, you may still catch a whiff of Kairouan's distinguished past as a fount of Arab poetry, calligraphy and doctrine. The chances are even better if you stay the night (see *Practical Information* for accommodation).

Start your tour by driving to the **Syndicat d'Initiative**, where you must sign an authorisation form and buy a ticket covering all the major holy sites. The office, next door to the tourist office (winter 8.30am–1pm and 3–5.45pm), is opposite Hotel Continental (signposted) on the Avenue de la République (the ring road), next door to the **Aghlabid Pools** (open-air site, accessible at all times).

These murky reservoirs have been pristinely restored and thus robbed of all clues to their 8th-century origins. The Aghlabids, who made Kairouan their capital (see *History and Culture*) built them to store water channelled from the Tell plateau by means of a 35-km (21-mile) aqueduct. Thanks to these, Kairouan was a garden city, in spite of its dustbowl setting.

Return to your car and drive along Rue Ibn el Jazzar (opposite the pools) to Bab el Tunis (the third in a string of arches). Here, turn left, following the sign for Hotel Marhala, Bir Barouta and the Zaouia of Sidi Abid el Ghari-

Excursions from Sousse

Gulf of Hammamet

40 km / 25 miles

• • • • Itinerary 8
• • • • Itinerary 9

Takrouna Enfidaville
Nadour
Hergla
Borj Trimiche Port el Kantaoui
Kalaâ Kebira Sousse
Sebkhet Kelbia Kalaâ Sghira
Monastir
Gulf of Monastir
Khniss
M'razig Ksar Hellal
Kairouan Moknine
Sebkhet Sidi el Hani Souk Saydi
Mahdia
Sebkhet ech Cherita Bou Merdés Ksour Essaf
El Jem
Chebba
Souk Hibira Sebkhet el Gherra
El Hencha

ani, weaving through Avenue Habib Bourguiba, the main artery of the medina, to Bab ech Chouhada. Park your car (small charge) on the gate's far side.

My proposed walking tour of the **medina** is circular, aiming for the Great Mosque, but dipping into minor mosques and sights en route. Begin by walking back through Bab ech Chouhada and proceed for about 50m (50yds) towards a mosque which doubles as a prop for rugs and carpets. Take the small street to the right of the mosque and stop at the first gate on the right, the entrance to the

14th-century **Zaouia of Sidi Abid el Ghariani**, a complex of elaborately tiled and carved chambers centring on the caged tomb of the Sufi teacher.

Out of the *zaouia*, follow the road round to the left, bearing right at a T-junction, towards the 9th-century **Mosque of the Three Doors**, passing carpentry workshops on the right and weavers on the left. The mosque (closed to visitors) is identified by the lovely bands of calligraphy – verses from the Koran – over its three doors. At one time it was a base of the Assiou brotherhood, a Sufi sect known throughout North Africa for violent, trance-induced rituals (now outlawed).

From here turn down Rue Moulay Taieb, directly opposite the three doors. This leads into a small *place*. Take the first right off the *place* and at the next junction go left through an arch and proceed through a quiet residential

Inside the Great Mosque

area. At the next mosque fork right. This leads to Rue Ibrahim Ibn el Aghlab and the fortress walls of the 9th-century **Great Mosque** (8am–3pm, Fri 8am–12.30pm, closed during prayer times). Walk left for 150m/yds to the mosque's main gate.

Inside, cross the *sahn* to the prayer-hall on the right. Non-Muslims are not permitted inside, but there are good views through the magnificent cedar doors. A forest of Roman pillars, re-employed for a new faith, are lit by thousands of tiny lamps. The handsome blue and white carpet, whose design allocates a precise amount of space to each worshipper, was a gift from Saudi Arabia. Through the main, central door you can see the gorgeously ornamented *mihrab* (niche indicating the direction of Mecca), the handiwork of faïence-makers in 9th-century Baghdad, and, to its right, the world's oldest *minbar* (from which the *imam* leads prayer). The marble *sahn* (courtyard) was designed on a slope so that rainwater could be channelled into a decanting drain and thence to an underground cistern, necessary not only for ritual ablutions but also as a water supply in times of siege when the mosque was a place of refuge for the populace. It is overlooked by the sturdy, battlemented minaret.

Turn right out of the mosque and at the main road turn left. Over on the right are the whitewashed tombs of the Cemetery of the Shorfa, descendants of the Prophet (derived from the Arab word *shouf*, to see). After passing the kasbah, turn left past the Café Arabica to reach **Bab el Tunis**. Turn left into Avenue Habib Bourguiba (which you drove down earlier), with its eye-catching goods and pungent produce. If you want to picnic in the Mosque of the Barber, which we visit later (not as sacrilegious as it sounds), pick up supplies here. If not, there are several simple restaurants where you can lunch on salad *mechouia*, kebabs or *brik a l'oueuf*. First, though, explore the covered souks, a shady warren of cupboard-sized workshops where traditional industries still thrive, by striking left just past the sign for Fairouz restaurant. Also here, is **Bir Barouta**, a depressing tourist trap, where a blinkered camel pumps water from a well. According to local legend, this is the source which prompted Oqba Ibn Nafaa to found the city (see *History and Culture*). You can sample the holy water for a tip.

Rejoining Avenue Habib Bourguiba, pause for a coffee on the triangular terrace of **Café Halfouine**, a hub of social intercourse in the medina, and afterwards, on the way back to Bab ech Chouhada, dip into **Meilleur Makrouth**, a stylish shop devoted to *makrouth*, sticky cigar-shaped pastries filled with date or fig paste.

For the **Mosque of the Barber** (7.30am–6pm), also known as the

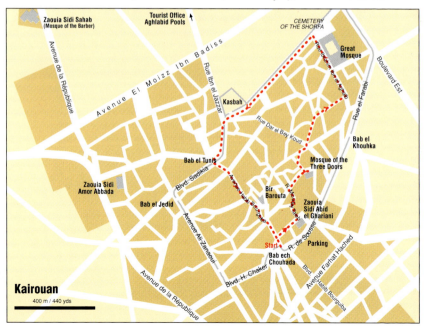

Kairouan

400 m / 440 yds

The Mosque of the Barber

Zaouia of Sidi Sahab (Companion of the Prophet), regain your car at Bab ech Chouhada and head for the Tunis road via the Nouvelle Ville. The mosque, a sprawling white building signposted Mausoleum of Abdu Zamu el Balawi, is on the left-hand side of Avenue de la République as you leave town.

This is one of the loveliest shrines in Tunisia, lavishly tiled in stylised arch, urn and plant motifs and topped by canopies of lacy stucco. The tomb, ornately caged in the central chamber (remove shoes to visit), is a magnet for pilgrims. Sidi Sahab, equivalent in Christian terms to one of Christ's apostles, was dubbed the Barber on account of three whiskers from the Prophet's beard which he always carried. Take your lunch inside the *zaouia*: providing you are discreet, nobody will mind if you join the pilgrims picnicking in the cool and airy antechambers.

Takrouna resident

To return to Sousse via the perched Berber village of Takrouna, take the Tunis road to Enfidaville. When you reach the main Tunis to Sousse road (after approximately 60km/35 miles) turn left towards Tunis and shortly afterwards make another left to Zaghouan (signposted). The road passes two Christian cemeteries, the crumbling and vandalised colonial cemetery and, furthest from the road, the well-kept Commonwealth War Cemetery containing the graves of 1,551 British and Commonwealth soldiers who fell during the last months of the Tunisian Campaign of World War II.

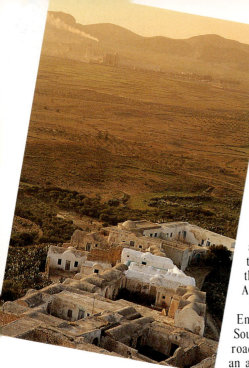
Takrouna views

Takrouna (sign-posted) is 2km (1 mile) left of the Zaghouan road. Piled on an outcrop of rock on the Enfidaville plain, this rugged eyrie was the Germans' penultimate line of defence in the Tunisian Campaign of 1943. Braving the barrage of women kitted out in Berber finery, get out of your car to admire the view. The best vantage point is a ledge behind the tomb of local holy man Sidi Ali Bou Khadida.

From here, drive back to Enfidaville and the road to Sousse, branching off for the coast road at the signpost for Hergla, an attractive whitewashed village with an 18th-century mosque dedicated to Sidi Bou Mendel, a Hergla man who, according to legend, sailed to Mecca on a handkerchief. The road hugs the shore, offering opportunities for a late afternoon swim. Stop at **Port el Kantaoui**, a self-contained tourist resort built with Gulf Arab funds on a virgin stretch of coast in the 1970s. The contrast with Kairouan couldn't be greater. Potter round its marina, rent a pedalo, have a cappuccino in one of the cafés on the quay or stay and have supper. From here, it is a straightforward run back to Sousse.

9. El Jem

To the Roman amphitheatre at El Jem via Monastir, Bourguiba's birthplace, and Mahdia, the Fatimid capital. See map on p. 52.

This itinerary is designed as a full-day tour from Sousse, but if time is short (or you are based in Monastir) concentrate on El Jem, the sixth largest amphitheatre in the Roman world. A car is recommended if you want to see Mahdia, but Monastir and El Jem can be reached by train (Sousse's port-side station for Monastir; its main station on Boulevard Hassouna Ayachi for El Jem).

Take the main road to Monastir rather than the coast road, which save for the *zone touristique* (hotel strip) is depressingly ugly. Signposts lead you into town, delivering you at the old city walls. Circumvent the walls (keeping them on your left). At a gold statue of Habib Bourguiba, Monastir's most famous son, turn left and proceed towards the domes and minarets of the **Bourguiba family mau-**

Mausoleum at Monastir

soleum where Tunisia's first president is buried. Take the second right past the ONAT shop and park.

You can walk into the extensive grounds of the mausoleum to take a closer look at the multi-million dinar edifice, expanded and embellished almost constantly during Bourguiba's last years as president. The cemetery's more modest whitewashed tombs and *koubbas* inspired Paul Klee's *Red and White Domes*.

Afterwards adjourn to the **Ribat of Harthema** (Tues–Sun, winter 8.30am–5.30pm, summer 8am–7pm, closed Mon), on the shore opposite the mausoleum. Like the one in Sousse, it dates from the early years of Arab expansion (in this case the 8th century), when it served as a base from which *murabatin*, warrior-monks, could launch *jihads*.

From Monastir, proceed to **Mahdia**. To find the right road, drive along Monastir's beach to the port, from where it is signposted. The stretch between Monastir and Mahdia is where the expanding towns and villages of the Sahel collide. As you approach Mahdia, follow signs for *centre ville*, effectively keeping to the corniche. Park outside the Skifa el Kalaa (signposted), at one time the sole entrance to the capital of the Fatimids (before the dynasty moved its base to Cairo in 973). Before penetrating its massive walls, have a fish or kebab lunch at **Le Quai** or the better **Lido**, almost next to one another on the main road overlooking the port.

For an after-lunch coffee, retire to the sleepy **Place du Caire** on Rue Oubad Attat el Methi, through the Skifa el Kalaa (black passage). This shady square is overlooked by the tiled gateway of the Hajji Mustafa Hamza Mosque, whose hours of prayer are the only interruptions to rouse the card-playing, tea-swigging locals. Look out for silk weavers in workshops off the Rue Oubad Attat. On a Friday, you may be able to buy their work in Mahdia's weekly market.

Mahdia

In order to leave plenty of time for **El Jem**, aim to leave Mahdia by 2pm. The route is straightforward. Take the coastal road towards Ksour Essaf. Just before you get to it, branch right, cutting through an unbroken landscape of olive groves, source of the region's wealth since Carthaginian times. After some 30km (18 miles), you will see El Jem's **amphitheatre** (summer 7am–7pm and winter 8am–5.30pm; admission fee) rearing out of the modern town, much of which was built with the amphitheatre's yellow stone. To get to the entrance, cross the railway line and turn right along Avenue Habib Bourguiba at Hotel Julius.

Built in 230 as a copy of the Coliseum in Rome, the amphitheatre served the growing town of Thysdrus, which by the 3rd century had a population of 10,000 and was the richest city in North Africa. Its three tiers – you can climb to the top – could accommodate over 30,000 spectators. Partial restoration shows how it looked; the marble seating closest to the action was for the city's elite, while the rougher hewn pews were for the plebs.

Beneath the arena are the chambers and passages where the gladiators, charioteers, beasts and victims waited their turn. On the evening before combat, the gladiators would hold a banquet, a merry occasion, as shown by a mosaic from El Jem now in the Bardo in which a party of carousing gladiators is captioned *Silentium dormiant tauri* ('silence the bulls sleep').

Years after the decline of Roman Thysdrus, El Jem was the Berbers' last bastion against the Arab invaders.

Before leaving El Jem, drop into the excellent museum (just past Hotel Julius on the road to Sfax; same hours as the amphitheatre), containing the many mosaics, inscriptions and statues that could not squeeze into the Bardo or the archaeological museum in Sousse. Then take the main, inland road back to Sousse.

Amphitheatre at El Jem

The Oases

Southern Tunisia starts with the pink hills of the Jerid. South of here lie the *chotts* (crystallised salt lakes) of which the Chott el Jerid is by far the most well known, palm oases, troglodyte villages, *ksour* (the strongholds of the tribes) and the island of Jerba (see section on *Jerba and the Ksour*).

Most tour companies now run two- or three-day 'desert excursions' from coastal resorts for around £80–120 ($120–180), depending on whether travel is by coach or in a convoy of 7-passenger jeeps (these do not go anywhere that an ordinary small car couldn't handle). However, since package excursions defeat most of the appeal of the south, it is worth travelling independently. Shared between two people travelling together, costs (hotels, food and hire of a small car) are only fractionally more. Either way, see *Practical Information* for advice on travelling in desert regions.

The ochre-coloured town of Tozeur makes a good base for exploring the oases and the *chotts*. It has hotels at all levels and a strong Saharan feel. It is famous for its dates

Oasis personnel

and fancy, geometric brickwork. A lush palmerie on the southern edge of town (near most of the hotels) invites cool walks and songbirds. Alternatively, you could hike up to the Belvedere (signposted at the far end of Avenue abou el Kacem Chebbi) for views over the palmerie and *chott* and a dip in one of Tozeur's 200 springs.

The three itineraries which follow are all based on Tozeur.

59

10. Mountain Oases

Through the Selja Gorge on the Lézard Rouge train; a circuit by car of the mountain oases of Tamerza and Chebika.

This is designed as a day trip, but you could stay the night in Tamerza (see Practical Information *for accommodation) and spend the following morning hiking or riding a donkey to Mides, a third mountain oasis, on the Algerian border. Note: past Tamerza the road is unsurfaced in places.*

To get to Metlaoui (50km/30 miles), the dusty mining town where we start this tour, leave Tozeur no later than 9.45am on the Gafsa road. In Metlaoui, the railway station is off to the left before the road crosses the railway line on the Gafsa side of town.

Le Lézard Rouge, an old beyical train, leaves Metlaoui for the Selja Gorge at 11am every day except Monday. The appeal of the trip is the old-fashioned charm of the train combined with dramatic scenery. The train stops at the most spectacular part of the gorge, allowing passengers a brief wander round before chugging back at 12.30pm. Fellow passengers are mainly tourists, but the ride is also popular with Tunisian newly-weds.

Back in Metlaoui, regain your car, top up its tank and take the road to Tamerza (backtrack towards the Tozeur end of Metlaoui and branch right), climbing into the heart of phosphate mining country. At Moulares – 'mother of brides' – follow the sign for Redeyef, where the pink phosphate dust settles, and thence along the back of gloriously scenic uplands to Tamerza (signposted Tamaghza), 24km (15 miles) further on. At Ain el Karma the road joins Oued el Horchane, dry in summer but a potential torrent in winter months. At **Tamerza**, rest at the upmarket Tamerza Palace Hotel,

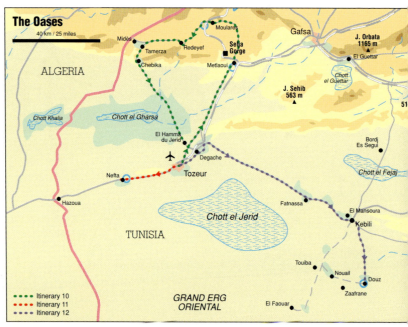

The Oases

40 km / 25 miles

Moulares

Gafsa

J. Orbata
1165 m

Mides

Redeyef

Selja
Gorge

El Guettar

Tamerza

ALGERIA

Chebika

Metlaoui

Chott
el Guettar

J. Sehib
563 m

51

Chott Khalia

Chott el Gharsa

El Hamma
du Jerid

Bordj
Es Segui

Degache

Chott el Fejaj

Nefta

Tozeur

Hazoua

Fatnassa

El Mansoura

Kebili

Chott el Jerid

TUNISIA

Touiba

Nouail

Douz

Zaafrane

GRAND ERG
ORIENTAL

El Faouar

● ● ● Itinerary 10
● ● ● Itinerary 11
● ● ● Itinerary 12

Chebika

which overlooks the crumbling *pisé* (mud and palm fibre) ruins of old Tamerza. Have lunch or a drink by its pool. Afterwards drive through new Tamerza and turn left for '*la grande cascade de palmerie*', reached through the grounds of Hôtel des Cascades. A small café above the falls is a shady spot in which to take tea.

Between Tamerza and Chebika the road declines to the plain. **Chebika**, stacked into the escarpment off to the left of the road, offers similar attractions to Tamerza: a waterfall, palmerie and low-key cafés.

From here the road crosses the periphery of the Chott el Gharsa – not as spectacular as the Chott el Jerid (see *itinerary 12*) – rejoining the main road outside Tozeur. Stop off at **Café de l'Indépendence** on Avenue Habib Bourguiba for a late afternoon *café au lait*.

11. Sunset over Nefta

A late afternoon drive to the holy oasis of Nefta.

Leave Tozeur from Avenue Farhat Hached. It is a 28-km (17-mile) ride to Nefta, along a straight but undulating stretch of road visited by gusts of sand and herds of goats and camels.

Nefta is famous for Sufi mystics and sunsets. The best place to catch the latter is from **Café de la Corbeille**, on the rim of an enormous 'basket' (*corbeille*) of palms protected from the sandy blast of the Grand Erg Oriental by the enclosing escarpment. To find it, turn right off the main street as you enter town, following signs for Hôtel Mirage. The road skirts the top of the 'basket', ending up at the café, next to the hotel (the coach parties don't stay long, so don't be put off by crowds). Prepare to be mobbed by children as you arrive.

Installing yourself at one of the ring-side tables on the café's terrace, sit back to watch the sun sink behind a band of domes. Nightfall begins with the haunting call of the *muezzin*. The café serves beer and wine, and is hence a draw to locals. After dark, it converts into a friendly grill serving good, cheap food under the stars.

Nefta, famous for sunsets

A morning or afternoon drive over the Chott el Jerid to Douz. A good option for those en route to Jerba and the Ksour. (See Practical Information for accommodation in Douz.)

The **Chott el Jerid** is flat, barren but breathtaking: a thick, glittering crust of salt stretching as far as the eye can reach. The remains of a vast lake left behind when the Mediterranean retreated, it effectively cuts Tunisia in half. Crossing the chott used to be hazardous: Norman Douglas, who travelled in these parts in 1912, was apparently told how on one occasion the chott gulped up a caravan of 1,000 baggage camels.

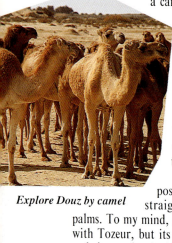

A perfectly safe causeway now crosses the chott. To get to its start, leave Tozeur on the Degache/Kebili road (signposted), taking the Kebili road from Degache.

Nothing disturbs the chott's white expanse, save for the mirages racing across its surface. Stop and take a closer look: beautifully cracked, it is like a frozen lake in winter. The only lifeform is a couple of café-cum-souvenir stalls which have sprouted midway along the causeway. Its far side is rimmed by dunes.

At Kebili (Tuesday souk), pick up the signposts for **Douz**, a further 30km (18 miles) along a straight and well-maintained road flanked by date

Explore Douz by camel

palms. To my mind, Douz, small and sandy, compares unfavourably with Tozeur, but its position, right on the edge of the Grand Erg, reels in tourists looking for *Lawrence of Arabia* landscapes, and hotels are spawning rapidly.

When you arrive, follow signs for the *zone touristique* through the palmerie. Eventually, you will see the well-trodden dunes off to the right, preceded by a huge herd of camels decked out for riding (waiting for custom from the coaches). Adjourn to Hotel Mehari for lunch. If you want to explore the small oases around Douz by camel, either in the afternoon or the following day, enquire at the Tourist Office, which will make arrangements on your behalf, or negotiate directly with one of the cameleers.

The Chott el Jerid

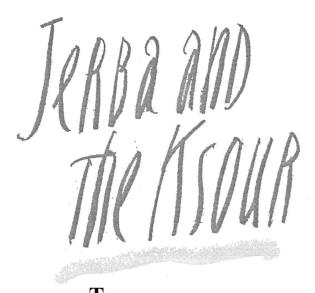

Jerba and the Ksour

The island of Jerba is flat and dry but bushy-topped. It is a contender for Homer's Land of the Lotus Eaters and, since hotel development in the 1970s, a magnet for more modern hedonists too. Yet in spite of package holidaymakers and the island's tiny size (29km/18 miles by 27km/16 miles), its distinctive culture remains intact.

Shortly after the Arab conquest Jerba was a hotbed of Kharijitism, a fiercely puritanical strand of Islam. Though the movement was extinguished on the mainland by the 9th century, pockets survived on Jerba. To this day, Jerbans are known for their piety, and the island is said to have 246 mosques. Buttressed, and rounded by centuries of whitewash, they are some of the most intriguing buildings in Tunisia. An ancient and once large Jewish settlement has plummeted since independence, but old retainers man the synagogue at El Ghriba and can be seen wandering round Houmt Souk in baggy trousers.

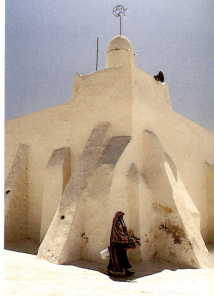

Jerba, island of mosques

I have devised two tours of Jerba: a walking tour of Houmt Souk and a moped ride into the interior. Following these are two motoring tours on the southeast mainland, the first from Jerba to the troglodyte village of Matmata and the second a leisurely potter round the *ksour*, the perched and fortified villages. This second tour is designed to depart from Tataouine but could be managed in a longish day from Jerba.

63

13. Jerba's 'Capital'

A morning walk in Houmt Souk, beginning on Place Hedi Chaker.

Begin the morning with a coffee at **Café Zarraa** on Houmt Souk's Place Hedi Chaker, the pretty central square. Afterwards take Rue Mohammed Ferjani off the square (passing Hotel Jerba Erriad), turning left at its end then immediately right, passing the Hôtel Sables d'Or and eventually reaching a shady crossroads. On the left, notice the top of the old French church – now a fitness club – which once catered to European merchants. Bending round to the left, you pass the **Mosque of the Turks**, with its oasthouse-shaped minaret. At Rue du 2 Mars, turn right and walk along to the multi-domed **Mosque of the Stranger**, with its square minaret, and the **Zaouia of Sidi Brahim**

Traffic, Jerba

with its tiled dome and loudspeaker popping out of the top (all of these are closed to non-Muslims).

As you walk up to the Mosque of the Stranger, look out for Touring Club du Tunisie's **Hotel Marhala** on the right (entrance is to the right through an arch), an old *fondouk* (merchants' lodging-house) which has been turned into a modest but pleasant hotel.

Turn left at Atlas Voyages Tunisie just in front of the Mosque of the Stranger, passing Restaurant Ettebsi, a good option for lunch later, and Mattei car hire (as a rule cheaper than Hertz, Europcar, etc). Turn right at Hotel Essaada, passing a large leatherwear shop on the right. Just past the hotel, on Avenue Abdelhamid el Cadhi, is the town **museum** (summer 9.30am–4.30pm, winter 8am–noon and 3–7pm, closed Fri; admission fee), housed in a crumbling 18th-century tomb. It provides an excellent introduction to Jerba, shedding light on the island's Kharijite and Jewish past, its varied costumes, furniture and crafts.

Leaving the museum, turn right and retrace your steps to Hotel Essada. Continuing in the same direction, walk down Rue Habib Thameur which will deliver you back at the Mosque of the Turks.

If you have the energy and time, take a look at the **Borj el Kebir** (8am–6pm; closed Fri; admission fee), at the end of Rue Taieb Mehri (north of the Mosque of the Turks). Draghut, 'the drawn sword of Islam', routed the Spanish from this fort in 1560. He massacred the occupants, piling 500 skulls in a heap on the shore, where they stayed until 1848.

En route is the site of the island's main market on Mondays and Thursdays (Houmt Souk is Arabic for marketplace) – far more interesting than the Aladdin's cave bazaars in the centre of town.

14. Twin Faiths

A day's moped ride through Jerba to El Ghriba Synagogue at Er Riadh and the mosque at El May, returning via the coast. Finish the day with a Turkish bath in Houmt Souk.

Mopeds (and cycles) can be hired from opposite the Restaurant Ettebsi on Rue Habib Thameur in Houmt Souk and from the big hotels. Pack a picnic and a bathing costume.

Leave Houmt Souk via Avenue Habib Bourguiba, passing Tunis Air on your right. The turning to Er Riadh (signposted right) is 6km (4 miles) from the capital. El Ghriba is signposted off to the left as you approach the village, at the top of a short road.

El Ghriba (summer 7am–6pm, winter 9.30am– 4.30pm; closed Saturday) is a place of pilgrimage for Jews worldwide. Although the current buildings are 20th-century, El Ghriba's origins are far older. Legend cites 600BC when a holy stone fell from heaven and a mysterious girl materialised to direct the building of a temple. The interior (headgear supplied for visitors) is surprisingly brightly painted and tiled. One of the keepers shows visitors round, directing them to an ancient Torah and the place where weddings are held (rarely these days). A donation is more or less obligatory.

Leaving the synagogue, return to

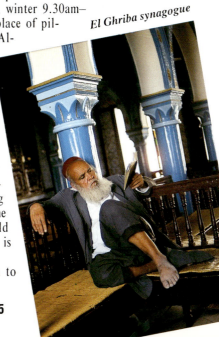

El Ghriba synagogue

Er Riadh, known as Hara es Seghira (little ghetto) when it was the heart of Jerba's Jewish community, and from there back to the main Houmt Souk-El Kantara road. Turn right to **El May** (about 4km/2½ miles). Its mosque – heavily buttressed, with a thimble-shaped minaret and seeming to melt in a surfeit of whitewash – is on the left as you enter town (past the Total station).

Carry on to **Midoun** (first left past the mosque), a much quieter journey between citrus and olive groves, farms and wells, which offers opportunities to unpack your picnic and bathing costume from the top box. Stop for tea in the centre of Midoun.

Afterwards carry on to the coast and take the *zone touristique* (hotel strip) back to Houmt Souk. For bathing, look out for signs to the *plage publique* by Hotel Penelope, one of the few stretches that hasn't been colonised by a hotel.

Back in Houmt Souk, sluice out the dust of the open road with a Turkish bath. There are several dotted about. Women can try **Hammam Sidi Brahim** (open for men 5.30am–12noon and for women 1–6pm) on rue de Bizerte next to the taxi stop in Sidi Brahim Square. Men should ask staff at their hotel to direct them to a *hamam* open to men in the afternoon.

15. Troglodyte Village

A drive from Jerba to the troglodyte village of Matmata and thence to Tamezret. See map on p. 64.

Leave late morning, aiming to return to Jerba late afternoon/early evening, when the setting sun brings out the pink and amber tints of the Jebel Dahar. If you want to spend the night in a troglodyte hotel – a good idea if you are planning to go on to Tozeur – see Practical Information *for options.*

Catch the ferry from Ajim (every 15 minutes during summer) and at Jorf take the road to Mareth and then to Gabes, turning off to Matmata a few kilometres outside town.

From Gabes the road to **Matmata** climbs into the Jebel Dahar, a tussocky, rugged landscape relieved by white-domed *koubbas* (tombs of holy men) and spiked by palms. Look out for cave dwellings excavated from the escarpment. After about 30km (18 miles) it reaches new Matmata, where old Matmata's residents were re-housed in the wake of President Bourguiba's misguided campaign to 'efface the mud huts, which mar our countryside, and rid our local population and tourists from this depressing sight'.

Fortunately for George Lucas and Stephen Spielberg, who used Matmata as a location in *Star Wars* and *Raiders of the Lost Ark*, enterprising locals had a better grasp of what tourists like and the original Matmata, 9km (5 miles) further on, was preserved to become a major tourist sight. Its lunar land-scape, marred by some overground build-ings, appears shortly after a '*Bienvenue*' notice which has been picked out in stones on the hillside.

At Matmata, park near Hotel Marhala and wander round, peering into the pits (living quarters are excavated in their sides). Pesky children may press you to go inside; if you take up their offers – and since you have come this far, why not? – expect to give a sizeable tip. There are cafés round about, and all the troglodyte hotels serve lunch.

Afterwards, make for the stone village of **Tamezret** (10km/6 miles), signposted off to the left as you leave Matmata. This Berber stronghold is much less visited than Matmata and the road there affords many delightful vistas. The village has a café of sorts.

Troglodyte transport, Matmata

Return to Jerba the way you came (sadly, Gabes , now an industrial centre, doesn't merit a stop), taking time to admire the views. If you are hungry, stop off for a quick dinner at one of the grill-cafés that line the road near Mareth. They cater to traffic to and from Libya, and their meat, often lamb, is invariably fresh and succulent.

Cave life pictured at Matmata

16. Sampling the Ksour

A circular tour from Tataouine to Chenini and Douirat. Vehicle essential. See map on p. 64.

The route to Chenini (20km/12 miles) is signposted from the back of Tataouine. If you are coming into Tataouine from Jerba, turn right at Hotel Ennour. The road is good to Chenini but becomes difficult – take it slowly – from there to Douirat.

A new village has been built in the valley below old **Chenini**, but many villagers persist, out of necessity or preference, to live in the original settlement. Despite its lovely setting, new Chenini is non-descript, making old Chenini, piled high into a U-shaped spur, its white mosque sitting on the saddle in-between, all the more magnificent. It comes into sight as you climb away from the new village and turn the corner.

Most villagers live on the right-hand side of the spur, but the crumbling left leg is well worth a closer look. Park the car by the café/restaurant, and proceed along the well-trodden path, snaking rather than climbing to the top. For interesting insights into this Berber-speaking community, engage the services of one of the local boys who gather outside the café.

Looking down, you can examine the construction of the *ksour*. As elsewhere in the region, rows of caves are excavated along the rock's softer strata. They are fronted by courtyards and shielded from the public pathways by *ghorfas* (barrel-shaped outhouses used for storage), the backs of which double as walls. Inside the living quarters look for 'hands' and other symbols to repel the evil eye. Also watch out for abandoned olive presses and black stains where the olive sediment has been tipped.

Returning to the bottom, have a soft drink in the café and then proceed to **Douirat** (20km/12 miles) by turning left (the only option apart from returning the way you came). As this route is un-surfaced, proceed only if your tyres, including the spare, are good. At 6km (4 miles) the road forks: be sure to take the left route to El Chott (the right route to Ksar Ghilane is for 4-wheel-drive vehicles only). The pleasure of this section of the route is the scenery – dun-coloured hills cradling olive and fig trees – and the lack of fellow tourists. Douirat is similar to Chenini but abandoned. It is stacked into a cone-shaped outcrop, and camouflaged save for its whitewashed mosque. Its once extensive population – notice the forest of headstones at its foot – is now reduced to eight.

The tarmac road from Douirat leads you directly back to **Tataouine**, where you can eat at Hôtel La Gazelle or at one of several cheap *gargottes*.

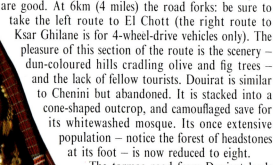

Traditional style

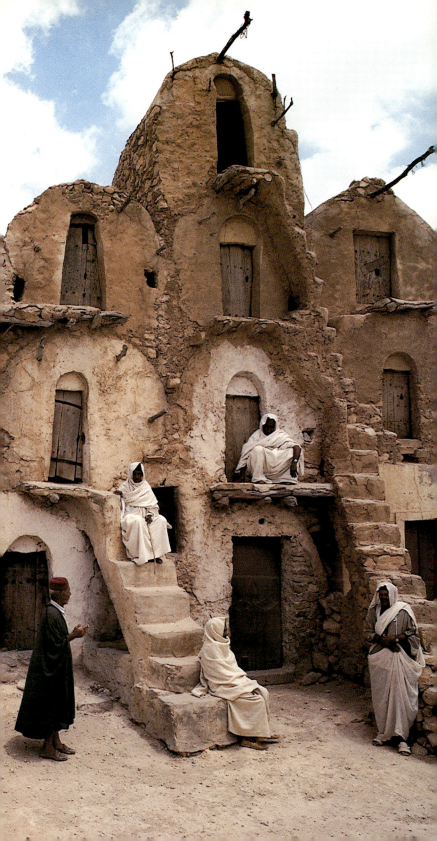

Shopping

In the tourist centres, souvenirs have edged out quality Tunisian crafts. Some of the items on sale – bags, jackets and brassware – are even imported from abroad, witness the Friday 'camel' market at Nabeul on Cap Bon. Each week tourists are bussed in from Sousse and Hammamet, and the market has now expanded into a vast pan-Arab bazaar carpeting a grid of streets on the eastern side of town (drift with the crowds to find it). Merchandise – toy camels are much more in evidence than the real thing – ranges from Egyptian papyrus to Moroccan *babouches* (slippers) and leather jackets. The sheer scale of the market seems to trigger shopping fever. To avoid expensive and easily-made mistakes, remember that items that look good in their North African setting often don't look as fetching in the average Western sitting-room.

To my mind, the best buys are coral from Tabarka, rugs (found everywhere) and the beautifully tooled wooden bowls sold around Ain Draham. Also attractive are the bulbous, filigree bird cages of Sidi Bou Saïd and the *rose de sable*, natural sculptures of crystallised gypsum excavated in the south.

Filigree bird cage

Whatever you buy, it is important to bargain hard. Begin bidding at approximately one-third of the asking price and settle at a fraction over half, though there are no fixed rules. Haggling for larger items, such as rugs or leather jackets, can be protracted and is invariably lubricated by copious quantities of tea or Boga lemonade. Prices are fixed in shops run by L'Office National de l'Artisanat Tunisien (ONAT), a government-run body which aims to promote Tunisian crafts.

In more upmarket shops, expensive purchases can be made by credit card: American Express, Visa and Mastercard are generally accepted.

Something for the kitchen?

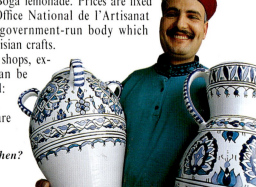

Jewellery

Tabarka's Avenue Habib Bourguiba is packed with shops selling coral jewellery, the carved and polished products of the coral harvested offshore. If you are serious about buying, take your time, browsing in each of the shops and asking for prices as you go. Examine clasps, as they are often clues to the level of workmanship.

More ethnic is silver Berber jewellery – brooches like stirrups, massive hoop earrings, chunky bracelets and *khul-khal*, heavy anklets, still worn by some older women in villages in the Sahel. Popular motifs are 'hands', designed to ward off the evil eye, and fish, a symbol of fertility since Roman times when a pisciform phallus was a common motif in mosaics.

Ethnic

Lighter work is found in Houmt Souk, Jerba and, in gold, in the labyrinthine jewellery souks off Souk el Attarine in the medina in Tunis. Much of Tunisia's silver jewellery is either influenced or produced by the Jewish jewellers of Jerba, who still serve as wholesalers to jewellers throughout the country. As a result, the jewellery souk in Jerba offers the best variety of jewellery, with some old pieces available.

Ceramics

Nabeul, near Hammamet on Cap Bon, Guellala on Jerba and Moknine near Monastir in the Sahel are all known for their potters, but you will find pretty much the same ware – painted and glazed ashtrays, plant holders, teapot stands and candlesticks – on sale all over the country. Among the most attractive and practical items, the huge earthenware pots and pitchers are difficult to transport, as are sufficient quantities of the lovely tiles which replicate the urn and plant designs found on mosque walls.

Carpets and Textiles

Though not bought as investments, Tunisian rugs are striking. The government monitors their production and sale and each one must have an official stamp stating whether it is *deuxième choix*, *première choix* or, top of the range, *qualité supérieure*. The more knots a carpet has to the square metre, the better it is. The number ranges from 10,000–490,000.

You are unlikely to find genuine antique articles for sale, but most ONAT shops have some on display. These can help you identify regional designs and develop an eye for quality. Kairouan is renowned for carpet-weaving, but the hard sell encountered here can be off-putting.

Also popular are *mergoums* (woven as opposed to knotted carpets). *Mergoums* from Gafsa and Gabes, but sold everywhere, are especially distinctive: they are usually distinguished by large, bright geometrical designs, sometimes incorporating naive images of camels and trees. They are fun for children's bedrooms. Much finer, darker patterns in wine-reds, browns, black and creams are particular to the *Ksour* region of the south.

Other textiles include 'marriage wraps' (though they would be just as attractive at an opera or a party), made in Mahdia, a town traditionally associated with silk weaving.

Wooden puppets

Brassware and Metalwork

Most of this is pretty ghastly, with pictures of mosques, camels, palm trees, gazelles and the names of resorts taking the place of traditional calligraphy and abstract patterns. If you want something good, go to the more up-market bazaars and antique shops (try Bazaar ed Dar, 8 Rue Sidi ben Arous, Tunis, or Boutique des Amisin, 55 Souk el Leffa, Tunis).

Spices , Sweets and other Edibles

Spice stalls-cum-herbalists are great draws to cooks and hypochondriacs alike. Most spices have a role in traditional medicine – for example, absinthe for liver complaints, cloves for toothache, cardamon to aid digestion, aniseed to sharpen the intellect and a whole bouquet of spices and herbs (as well as more arcane ingredients) to treat sterility and impotence.

The key spices in Tunisian cooking are saffron, cumin, sweet and hot red peppers and cinnamon. Good buys to take home are saffron, relatively cheap in Tunisia, and *rass el hanout* (shop-keeper's choice), a blend of 13 different spices.

Tunisian pastries makes a good gift for the sweet-toothed. For *makrouth* (pastry rolls filled with date or fig paste) you can't beat Meilleur Makrouth, inside the Bab ech Chouahada in Kairouan (see *itinerary 8*). For sticky pastries oozing with honey, pistachios and almond paste, try Madame Zarrouk, 41–43 Rue Echem, Tunis.

Antiquities

At all the main archaeological sites, expect to be approached by someone unwrapping a statuette, oil lamp or cache of muddy coins

Selling baskets in Tozeur

– quite often the custodian himself. Items are occasionally genuine, but if they are, they won't be cheap. It is forbidden by law to take true antiquities out of the country.

Leather Goods and Basketry

These include leather jackets, *babouches* (open-back slippers), handbags, backpacks, gold-incised pouffes, belts, wallets, etc. Slippers, wallets and dufflebags, often with woven panels or embroidery, make welcome presents. Baskets abound, often embroidered with abstract designs of flower, palm or camel motifs. Rush mats, made out of dwarf palm and esparto grass, make attractive runners, but they are traditionally used to line walls for winter warmth.

Woodwork

Carved olive wood bowls, chess boards and boxes are found in the Sahel, the centre of olive production. Ain Draham in the Khroumiria is also a good place to buy beautifully coloured thuya wood. Check hinges and clasps on boxes before buying. In the resorts you'll also find wooden, painted Saracen puppets.

Fossils and Crystals

As well as *rose de sable*, mentioned in the introduction, look out for fossils and, on the face of it, ordinary-looking chunks of rock packed with crystals.

Meilleur Makrouth, Kairouan

Eating Out

The best cooking is found in the home and, apart from in a few upmarket establishments in Tunis, most menus include only a small repertoire of Tunisian/North African specialities. As well as *couscous* (a meat or poultry and vegetable stew served on a bed of steamed semolina grains), look out for the specifically Tunisian *brik à l'oeuf* (a warm, deep-fried envelope of *maslouqua* [tissue-thin] pastry filled with runny egg, cumin, flat-leaf parsley, sometimes tuna or potato, and sprinkled with lemon juice), salad *mechouia* (a delicious purée of tomatoes, onions, roasted peppers and olive oil, served as a starter) and *kamounia*, a slow-cooked lamb, chicken or beef stew. All these are invariably accompanied by a small saucer of *haryssa*, a fiery pepper-based condiment that could blow an unsuspecting person's head off.

More basic fare includes *kefta* (spicy meatballs), liver and lamb kebabs, *chorba* (a thick vegetable soup, augmented by morsels of lamb, rice or pasta), *merguez* (beef sausages enlivened with sweet and hot red peppers) and *tajine*, which in Tunisia is similar to a Spanish omelette and not a *ragout* as it is in Morocco. Working-men's restaurants (*gargottes*) usually offer a range of these staples, plus one or two stews.

You may encounter sheep's head stew. This can be mouthwatering off the bone and with proper attention to refinements. Alas, the rough and ready version served in *gargottes* is not for the faint-hearted: a distinctly ovine skull, teeth still intact, rising out of an oily, tomato-based sauce.

Couscous, based on semolina grains

Upmarket restaurants concentrate on Mediterranean and French cuisine. Fish, often displayed with aplomb at the front of restaurants, is usually excellent, especially in Tunis and La Goulette (Tunis's port); but remember that its price is normally determined by weight, so it can work out to be expensive. Common types include *rouget* (red mullet), *merlan* (whiting), *loup de mer* (perch) and *thon* (tuna). A plate of *crevettes aioli* (prawns sautéed with garlic), crusty French bread and a glass of Celtia beer can be superb; also look out for fish couscous, especially on Jerba.

Sampling the varied produce of roadside vendors is one of the pleasures of touring by car. Verges are made more interesting by stalls and individuals selling fruit, freshly baked bread and occasionally crumbly curd cheese. Major routes, notably Medenine to Libya, are punctuated by grill restaurants, flagged by suspended legs of lamb and smoking braziers. A supper of salad *mechouia*, grilled lamb cutlets and *tabouna* (the flat, Tunisian bread), washed down with Safia mineral water, costs no more than 5D per head.

Alcohol, discouraged by the Koran, is available in licensed restaurants, some hotels and a few bars. The latter tend to be seedy outside the main resorts. Dependable wines (costing about 8D a bottle) include Coteaux de Carthage and Haut Mornag, both in red, white and rosé; Sidi Rais, a popular light rosé; and Muscat de Kelibi, a delicious golden-coloured wine. The Tunisian beer is Celtia and the local *eau-de-vie* is a palatable fig-based distilled wine called Boukha. Many hotel bars and restaurants do not serve alcohol during Ramadan; indeed, some close for the duration of the month-long daily fast. Spirits are comparatively expensive. A gin and Boga bitter lemon (invariably concertinaed to 'gin bugger' by bar staff) costs at least 5D.

Tea comes in a variety of guises, usually dark, sweet and stewed but more delightfully with mint or sprinkled with pine kernels (*thé aut pignons*). Coffee, too, is sometimes laced with orange flowers, cinnamon or cardamon, and occasionally blended with chocolate. *Café Turc* is Turkish coffee: sweet, black and silky in tiny cups. Italian *espresso* and *cappuccino* are also widely available in the resorts.

If you want your tea or coffee unsweetened, be sure to specify *sans sucre*. However, even the sternest denouncer of sugar may be tempted by Tunisia's sticky pastries: *baklawa* (a confection of almonds, honey and *maslouqua* pastry) and *makrouth* (a type of date or fig roll), popular in Ramadan and a speciality of Kairouan.

In the list of restaurants that follows, *$* = under 40 Dinars for two; *$$* = 40–70 Dinars for two; *$$$* = 70 Dinars plus for two. Prices include wine where it is available. Where booking is appropriate, telephone numbers are given.

A word of warning: there is no tradition of eating out in Tunisia and outside the capital and the big resorts good restaurants are scarce. Anyone travelling around will often rely on simple *gargottes*. Also, in spite of investment in tourism, service can be poor. Finally, apart from in the resorts, last orders are taken around 9–9.30pm.

Roadside dining

Tunis

Tunis has the largest selection of restaurants. All those mentioned here are licensed. For unbeatable value without alcohol (or chairs), try one of the stand-up rotisseries on Avenue Habib Bourguiba.

L'ASTRAGALE
17 Avenue Charles Nicolles
Tel: (71) 785080
Upmarket French restaurant. *$$$*

RESTAURANT DAR EL JELD
5 Rue Dar el Jeld
Tel: (71) 560916
Traditional cooking in a traditional town house. Recommended. Best to book. Closed on Sunday. *$$*

M'RABET
Souk el Trouk
Tel: (71) 263681
Built over the tombs of three holy men. Tunisian and international cuisine. Atmospheric coffee-house downstairs. *$$*

L'ORIENT
7 Rue Ali Bach-Hambra
Tel: (71) 242058
Personal favourite. Well-cooked French and Tunisian food. Opposite the offices of *La Presse*. *$$*

CHEZ NOUS
5 Rue de Marseille
Tel: (71) 243048
Intimate, with theatrical flavour. Popular with middle-class Tunisians.

Food is mainly international and French. If you like, opt for *tapas* in the tiny front bar. Best to book. *$$*

COSMOS
7 Rue Ibn Khaldoun
Tel: (71) 241610
Good value and popular with tourists and Tunisians alike. Good fish. *$–$$*

Sidi Bou Saïd

Ayyam Zaman *($$$)*, **Zarrouk** *($$)*, both in the centre of the village, and **Le Pirate** *($$)*, down by the harbour on the other side of Sidi Bou, are the best. More basic is **Chargui**. All have garden restaurants.

Hammamet

Plenty of restaurants to choose from (along the corniche and in the Centre Commercial) but many are overpriced and not that good. Recommendations include **Chez Achouar** *($$)*, on Rue Ali Belhouène, for fish and seafood, and **Restaurant de la Poste** *($)*. **Pomo d'Oro** *($$)*, 6 Avenue Bourguiba, serves good Italian food. Opposite the Cultural Centre on Avenue des Nations Unies, is the **Restaurant du Théâtre** *($$)*.

Fresh ingredients

Bizerte

Le Petit Mousse
To my mind, the only place to eat in town. Delicious food (fish a speciality) at reasonable prices (*$$*). Sit inside or on the terrace. There is also a pizzeria in the garden (*$*).

Tabarka

Plenty of *gargottes*, some of which offer fish. For a licensed meal, head for the hotels or **La Montaza** (*$–$$*) on Avenue Habib Bourguiba.

Ain Draham

Hôtel Beau Sejour offers a cheap, if dull, *menu du jour* (*$*). **Hotel Rihana** (*$–$$*) is slightly better, but there is often a tour party installed.

El Kef

Several *gargottes*, but **Hotel Sicca Veneria** is the place to get a more elaborate meal with wine (*$–$$*).

Dougga

Again there are inexpensive grill restaurants in the centre of Teboursouk, but **Hotel Thugga** is the only licensed premises. Food is simple, but well-cooked and fresh (*$*).

Sousse

Like Hammamet, Sousse has a wide choice of restaurants. If you are staying for more than a few days, pick up recommendations from fellow tourists. Two good choices are **L'Escargot** (*$$*), 87 Route de la Corniche (tel: 73-224779 if you want a table on the terrace) and **Le Pacha** (*$$*), also Route de la Corniche (tel: 73-224 525). **Le Bonheur** (*$$*), tel: (73) 252742. Place Farhat Hached, does good grilled meat and fish.

Kairouan

A slim selection of restaurants for the number of tourists (most of whom eat at **La Fleur** [*$$*],on the Tunis road). **Le Roi de Couscous**, Rue du 20 Mars has a set menu and is popular with locals. For a simple meal with wine, try **Hotel Splendid** (*$$*) on Avenue du 9 Avril.

There are plenty of rotisseries in the new town, and sandwiches (French *batons* crammed with *merguez*/kebabs, olives, salad and chips) available late into the night from the stalls at the end of Avenue de la République.

Tozeur

Outside the hotels (the 5-star **Dar Cherait**, tel: 76-454 888, offers the best food) the only option for licensed dining are **Le Petit Prince** (*$–$$*) in the palmerie, signposted off Avenue Abou el Kacem Chabbi, and **Les Andalous** (*$$*) on the Route de Degache. Better value are the **Restaurant de la République**, off Avenue Habib Bourguiba, and **Restaurant du Sud**, on Avenue Farhat Hached (both under *$*).

L'Escargot at Sousse

Jerba

The best restaurant is the fish restaurant **Princesse de Haroun** (*$$–$$$*) near the harbour. Among a cluster of restaurants offering fish and Tunisian dishes on Place Hedi Chaker, the pretty square in the centre of town, **Restaurant du Sud** (*$$*) and **Baccar** (*$$*) are the best. More basic but good are **Les Palmiers** (*$*), rue Mohammed El Ferjani, and **Restaurant Berbère**, Place **Farhat Hached**.

Calendar of Special Events

Opposite are some of Tunisia's major celebrations, but you should check locally for exact dates. In addition to these, you may stumble upon small, village festivals in honour of local *marabouts* (holy men): a large encampment of tents usually indicates pilgrims.

The big Islamic celebrations are tied to the Hegira calendar and therefore moveable. The best known is Aid es Seghir, the feast marking the end of Ramadan. It is like Christmas but without the presents (though alms are given to the poor). Though this is a family occasion, the general ebullience rubs off on outsiders, especially in the evening when everyone strolls arm in arm through town. If you are anywhere near Tunis on Aid es Seghir, go to Sidi Bou Saïd, the most lively celebrant. Equally if not more important than Aid es Seghir is Aid el Kebhir, when families slaughter a sheep to commemorate Abraham's sacrifice. After the feast it is common to see sheepskins pegged out on roof-top terraces, along with entrails being dried for flavouring in winter stews.

Mouloud, the Prophet's birthday, is celebrated with particular panache in Kairouan.

On a more private scale still are weddings. Celebrations in the cities involve elaborate 'dos' in the big hotels, but in the countryside look out for processions of drum-beating men and ululating women, followed by donkeys or camels carrying the bride-price: furniture, flour, blocks of sugar, candles and cloth, with a calf for the feast bringing up the

Local celebration

MARCH/APRIL

Between April and May, when Cap Bon is drowned in the scent of orange blossom, orange festivals are held in Nabeul and Menzel Bouzelfa. However, their content tends to be educational rather than fun. Independence Day (20 March) is marked by nationwide parades.

MAY/JUNE

At El Haouaria on the tip of Cap Bon, the ancient Arab art of falconry is celebrated in May or early June, using young birds caught on their migration between Africa and Europe. Floats, fanfares and *fantasias* augment displays of falconry.

JULY/AUGUST

July and August are the main months for cultural events throughout Tunisia. Carthage holds a festival of drama in its restored Roman amphitheatre, while Hammamet's International Cultural Centre, in the grounds of George Sebastian's former villa, offers a packed programme of plays and concerts in its mock-Greek theatre near the beach. Every two years an amateur film festival is held in July at Kelibia on Cap Bon.

Sousse also puts on its glad-rags for the festival of Aoussou. This has a European flavour, with *papier-mâché* 'giants' and floats and an international theatre festival. More traditional diversions are offered at Testour's Festival of Mahlouf (a classical music imported from Moorish Spain between the 12th and 15th centuries), in which Tunisian musicians perform alongside ensembles from the rest of the Maghreb, the Middle East and Spain. Meanwhile Dougga's splendid amphitheatre is

the venue for an international festival of drama in July–August.

The Kerkennah islands hold the Festival la Sirene (sea mermaid) with folk music, parades, sports competitions and other activities (late July–early August).

SEPTEMBER/OCTOBER

Grombalia on Cap Bon holds a somewhat sober wine festival in September, with displays and exhibitions rather than bacchanalian carousing. In the South, autumn is equated with the date harvest; expect to find local date festivals all over the oases.

DECEMBER

The agricultural calendar draws to a close with the olive harvest, celebrated in Sfax, the capital of the Sahel.

The year is given a rousing send-off with the Festival of the Sahara at Douz, held in November or December (though it is occasionally held in January). The arena, complete with a modest grandstand, lies beyond the arch where the *zone touristique* peters out. Thousands of people gather to watch camel charging, *fantasias* (frenzied displays of horsemanship to the accompaniment of gunfire and sabre-waving) and folk dancing. This is Tunisia's most spectacular festival and it is worth making a special journey to see it. You should book accommodation in advance (there are several large hotels in Douz, and Kebili and Tozeur are within easy reach).

Also in December, the Oasis Festival at Tozeur is similar in content to the Festival of the Sahara, with *fantasias*, gunfire and camel racing.

See May/June for falconry

Practical Information

GETTING THERE

By Air

Tunisia's national airline, Tunis Air, operates direct flights to Tunis from London Heathrow Airport (four times a week) and most other principal European cities (but not from North America). Flying time from London is 2 hours 50 minutes. Apex tickets (booked in advance and non-transferable or refundable) cut

Have a good stay

prices considerably. (Contact Tunis Air, 24 Sackville Street, London W1S 3DS. Tel: 020-7734 7644.)

In addition, British Airways (Operated by GB Airways) runs five flights per week to Tunis from Gatwick (Tel: 0845-773 3377). Prices are roughly the same as those offered by Tunis Air.

In Britain, it is easy to find cheap charter flights. These normally fly to Monastir Skanes, but a few go to Sfax or Tunis.

There are no non-stop flights from the US. However, good connections can generally be made though Frankfurt, Paris and Rome in conjunction with trans-Atlantic carriers. Outside high summer, flights can often be found from the east coast for between $550–800 round trip.

By Sea

If you want to take your own vehicle with you to Tunisia, book well in advance, especially in high summer when migrant Tunisian workers drive through Europe to take the ferry for their annual holiday back home.

From Marseille to Tunis the journey takes 21–24 hours. To make a reservation from London, contact Southern Ferries, 179 Piccadilly, London W1V 9DB (Tel: 020-7491 4968). They also sail from Genoa.

From Trapani in Sicily the journey takes eight hours, from Naples via Cagliari and Trapani 45 hours and from La Spezia 21–24 hours. All arrive in Tunis. To book passage from Sardinia and Sicily, contact SMS Travel, 40 Kenway Road, London SW5 ORA (Tel: 020-7373 6548/9). To book passage from Naples, Trapani of La Spezia, contact Viamare Travel, Graphic House, 2 Sumatra Road, London NW6 1PU, tel: 020-7431 4560.

Between July and September the company Alscafi Bavigazione operates a jet-foil service between Trapani in Sicily and Kelibia on Cap Bon. The journey takes about three hours, but 'flights' are dependent on fine weather.

TRAVEL ESSENTIALS

Visas and Passports

EU, US and Canadian passport-holders do not require visas and are normally granted a stay of 90 days. Australian and New Zealand nationals require visas.

In Britain, for visa and passport enquiries, contact the visa section of the Tunisian Embassy, 29 Prince's Gate, London SW7 1QG, tel: 020-7584 8117.

Vaccinations

Unless you are arriving from a declared infected zone, no vaccinations are required by law. Some doctors advise taking precautions against cholera, polio and typhoid.

Customs

Duty-free allowances for visitors to Tunisia are (per person): 1 litre of spirits, 2 litres of wine, 400 cigarettes or 100 cigars or 500 grammes of tobacco, ¼ litre of perfume. Duty-free goods can be bought on arrival and departure.

Climate and When to Go

A Mediterranean climate – hot, dry summers and mild, wet winters – prevails in the north; desert conditions, with extremes of temperature (cold at night), prevail in the south.

Mid-summer temperatures can reach a fierce 50°C (122°F) around Medenine and Remada and over 40°C (104°F) along the coast, but more commonly hover around 37°C/98°F and 30°C/86°F respectively. Winter temperatures average 16°C (60°F) in Sousse, but 'beach weather' is unlikely from November to the end of March.

Good general times to go are late spring (May/June) or September/early October. During winter (November–February) the climate is unpredictable, but warmest in the south (Tozeur/Douz) and wettest in the north and along the coast.

Ramadan, the month-long time of fasting, has some disadvantages for travellers in less touristy regions, where cafés and restaurants close during the day and the sale of alcohol is suspended for the month. Tourists staying in the major resorts are unlikely to be affected by the fast.

Electricity

The electricity supply is 220 volts. Sockets and plugs are of the continental Europe variety, with two round pins.

Time Difference

Tunisian time is one hour ahead of Greenwich Mean Time, and six hours ahead of US Eastern time.

Religion plays a key role in society

GETTING ACQUAINTED

Religion

Tunisia is a tolerant Muslim country, but religion remains the biggest influence on society. The recent upsurge in Islamic fundamentalism is fuelled by economic problems and unemployment among the young (50 percent of students back the fundamentalists).

Faith makes five demands on a Muslim: the affirmation that there is no other god but God and Mohammed is his Prophet; prayer five times a day; the observance of Ramadan; the giving of alms to the poor, and a *haj* (pilgrimage) to Mecca at least once in a lifetime. Ramadan is a tradition as much as a religious obligation, and adhered to by almost everyone, regardless of whether or not they are 'good' Muslims.

A solid grounding in the Koran, believed to be the direct word of God

Change money?

revealed to the Prophet Mohammed, is considered a crucial part of a young child's education. Many pre-school children attend religious kindergartens where they learn the Koran's verses by rote.

Officially Tunisia follows the Sunni (orthodox) branch of Islam, but North Africa has a number of Sufi brotherhoods, which emphasise an ecstatic, mystical approach to God via trance and meditation. Nefta, west of Tozeur, is Tunisia's leading centre of Sufism.

How Not to Offend

Women shouldn't sunbathe topless on public beaches – though plenty of insensitive individuals do – and everyone should dress reasonably modestly (no shorts) in towns. Don't try to enter mosques unless it is clear that non-Muslims are admitted (when there will usually be an entrance fee). In *hammams*, it is customary to retain your underpants, though you will be stared at rather than expelled for removing them.

As a guest in a Tunisian home, observe two rules: remove shoes before venturing on to the carpets and never take alcohol as a gift unless you know your hosts intimately and know that it will be acceptable. During Ramadan refrain from eating, smoking or kissing/embracing in public during daylight hours.

MONEY MATTERS

The Tunisian dinar is divided into 1,000 millimes, which, somewhat confusingly, are occasionally called francs by the older generation. Recent official rates average 2D to £1 and 1.4D to $1. It is illegal to import or export dinars, but up to 30 percent of the money you have changed, up to a maximum of 100D, may be reconverted into hard currency. In remote areas, you may have trouble changing t r a v e l l e r ' s cheques.

To be on the safe side, and bearing in mind the limited opening hours of banks (see *Business Hours*), you should always keep enough money to last three days. Hotels offer the same rate of exchange as banks, but you cannot depend on a hotel changing money for you unless you are staying in it. You will generally get a better rate with cash than with travellers' cheques. In an emergency you may have to resort to the bank at the nearest airport, though even these may be closed if an international flight isn't due.

Credit cards are gaining acceptance in upmarket hotels and restaurants, and can be used to obtain money from main banks (you will have to pay interest on the sum from the day it is borrowed).

GETTING AROUND

Distances in Tunisia are short and public transport is well developed, so if you have plenty of time and little luggage travelling on a combination of trains, buses and *louages* (shared taxis) can be an effective way of seeing the country.

To and From the Airport

Trains and taxis operate from Monastir-Skanes airport, and buses (No 35) and taxis run from Tunis airport to the city centre. Buses run about every 30 minutes from 6am–9pm and take around 25 minutes. Independent travellers arriving in Sfax, which accepts some charter flights, may have to beg a lift into town on one of the tour operators' coaches, as there may not be any taxis available.

Domestic Flights

In addition to the international airports of Tunis and Monastir-Skanes, there are small airports at Sfax, Tozeur, Tabarka and Jerba. However, as distances are

Getting around

short, internal flights are unnecessary. If you plan to take domestic flights, get a timetable in advance as some routes have only one or two flights a week.

Taxis

For short journeys in towns take a *petit-taxi* (up to three passengers) or a *grand-taxi*, which are larger and more comfortable. Fares are metered. Between 9pm and 5am there is a 50 percent surcharge.

For journeys between towns I suggest you use *louages*, shared taxis (usually Peugeot station wagons), which are fast and effective and cost only slightly more than the bus or train. *Louage* stations are often found next to bus stations. Drivers call out their destination and set off as soon as they have the full complement of five passengers. To facilitate an early departure, you can pay the difference for the full amount of passengers, which is often quite nominal.

Trains

The SNCFT (Société Nationale des Chemins de Fer Tunisiens) runs four main routes from Tunis: north to Bizerte, south to Gabes via Hammamet, Sousse and Sfax and stations in between, west to Ghardimaou on the Algerian border via Beja and Jendouba, and southwest to Kalaat Kasbah via El Fahs.

Lines from Sousse and Sfax run west to the Algerian border, the latter running as far as Tozeur.

In addition, there are two light railways (*métro léger*): one between Tunis and La Marsa, which is ideal for visiting Carthage and Sidi Bou Saïd, and another running between Monastir and Sousse via the Monastir-Skanes airport.

Trains are inexpensive, clean and comfortable, often running to buffet facilities and air-conditioning in first class but they can be crowded. Stations can supply timetables on request, but for longer journeys it is advisable to arrive at least half an hour before departure in order to queue for a ticket and secure a seat.

Buy your ticket before boarding the train or you will pay double the fare. It is best to book in advance for the air-conditioned routes.

Buses

There is a wide network of bus routes operated by a variety of companies. The latter do not necessarily share the same station, so check which station you need in advance of travelling. Tunis bus station at Bab Alleoua is well organised with a central information unit. Travel by bus is cheap, and comfortable on longer routes.

Car Hire

Hiring a car is expensive. In summer and at Easter, when tourism is likely to be at its height, it is worth hiring in advance through one of the international companies (Budget or Europcar tend to be cheapest) before leaving home. Out of season, it is often better to hire locally and haggle over the price, particularly for periods of two weeks or more. Mattei is one of the cheapest local firms, with branches in all major towns. Four-wheel-drive vehicles for desert driving can be hired locally, usually with a chauffeur.

When you pick up your car, check its water and oil levels and make sure it has a good spare wheel and a jack (you will probably need them). Examine the insurance papers and be clear about exclusions.

Watch out for speed traps!

Always keep car documents and your passport with you when driving. Spot-checks are common, and you will be sent back to your base (or to the police station) if you drive without them. Watch out for speed traps on the outskirts of town. Speeding can result in an on-the-spot fine. Speed limits are 50kph (30mph) in urban areas, 90kph (56mph) on the open road and 110kph (68mph) on the

A typical hazard

Post Office opening hours

Summer:
Monday to Saturday 8am–1pm.
Winter:
Monday to Friday 8am–noon and 2–6pm,
Saturday 8am–noon.
In Ramadan:
If it falls in winter, Monday to Saturday
8am–3pm.
If it falls in summer, opening hours follow normal summer hours.

Public Holidays

State Holidays: New Year's Day; Anniversary of the Revolution – 18 January; Independence Day – 20 March; Youth Day – 21 March; Martyrs' Day – 9 April; Labour Day – 1 May; Republic Day – 25 July; Women's Day – 13 August, New Era Day – 7 November.

Religious holidays (governed by the Hegira calendar and therefore moveable): Aid es Seghir (day after the end of Ramadan); Aid el Kebhir (feast of the lamb); Muslim New Year; and Mouloud (the Prophet's birthday).

Market Days

The name of a village or town often reflects the day of its weekly souk: el Had

---

motorway. Be prepared to give lifts to policemen – not an unusual request.

Pay attention to parking restrictions, especially in Tunis and Houmt Souk, where clamping is common. Though penalties are low, waiting to be unclamped costs time.

Desert Driving

Off-piste desert driving is only recommended for the properly equipped (4-wheel-drive vehicle, experienced off-piste driver and guide) and even then only between October and May. In summer the intense heat can be hazardous. If you are planning to venture off the beaten track, you must inform the National Guard of your route and anticipated arrival time. Even on short journeys take plenty of water and some food. Most importantly, if you break down, stay with your vehicle and shelter in its shade.

HOURS & HOLIDAYS

Business Hours

Banks and post offices close on public holidays. Shops usually close for several hours at lunchtime – generally noon–4pm (3pm in winter), but then stay open until at least 7pm. During Ramadan shops always close in time for sunset, but re-open again later and trade late into the night.

Banks

Summer (mid-June to mid-September):
Monday to Friday 8–11am. Main tourist resorts usually have one bank which remains open outside these hours for exchange purposes only.
Winter (mid-September to 30 June):
Mon–Thur 7.30–11am and 2–4.15pm, Fri 8–11am and 1–3.15pm.
In Ramadan:
If it falls in winter, Monday to Friday 8–11.30am and 1–2.30pm.
If it falls in summer, opening hours are the same as normal summer hours.

Market day at Jerba

(Sunday); el Tnine (Monday); el Telata (Tuesday); el Arba (Wednesday); el Khemis (Thursday); el Jemma (Friday); es Sebt (Saturday).

ACCOMMODATION

Tunisia's hotels tend to be modern and bland, especially along the coast. There are no world-class grand hotels and suprisingly few French-inspired auberges. In the south, however, several old, traditional lodging-houses have been turned into stylish, if simple, small hotels, for example Hôtel des Sables d'Or on Jerba.

Hotels fall into six categories: 5-star luxe, 4-star, 3-star, 2-star, 1-star and unclassified. Expect private facilities in two-star hotels and above, but one-star hotels generally have at least a few rooms with bathrooms. Prices, posted in rooms, usually include a light breakfast. If you are a couple, be sure to establish whether the price you are quoted is per person or per room, especially in smaller hotels. It is often possible to get a list of hotels and tariffs from local tourist offices.

The following list of hotels is based on the towns and areas highlighted in this guide. In some places, particularly inland, there may be only one reasonable option. The following price codes – $ = under $30; $$ = under $100; $$$ = under $150; $$$$ = over $150 – are based on two people sharing a twin-bedded room in high season (the definition of high season depends on location: as a rule, it lasts longer in the seaside resorts). Half-board can be an attractive option in more remote regions. Apart from in Tunis, hotels are signposted.

Tunis

HOTEL ABOU NAWAS (5-star)
Avenue Mohammed V
Tel: (71) 350355; Fax: 352882
The city's only five-star hotel that offers the room sizes and amenities that five-star clients expect. $$$$

AFRICA EL MOURADI (5-star)
50 Avenue Habib Bourguiba
Tel: (71) 347477; Fax: 347432
This is Tunis's only high-rise building.

Conveniently situated on Avenue 7 Novembre in the heart of town. All amenities, including a cinema. $$$$

ORIENTAL PALACE HOTEL (5-star)
Avenue Jean Jaurès
Tel: (71) 348846; Fax: 350327
Newer and flashier than El Mouradi, but full five-star facilities, including an indoor swimming pool. $$$$

HOTEL MAJESTIC (3-star)
36 Avenue de Paris
Tel: (71) 332 666/848, Fax: 336 908
Colonial, 'wedding-cake' building. Lots of faded charm. Insist on a quiet room, away from the 'bridal salon', where noisy wedding receptions are held on most evenings. $$–$$$

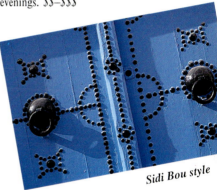

Sidi Bou style

CARLTON (3-star)
31 Avenue Bourguiba
Tel: (71) 330644; Fax: 71-338168
Comfortable, very well-run hotel in the heart of Tunis. $$$

HOTEL SALAMMBO (1-star)
6 Rue de Grèce
Tel: (71) 33425; Fax: 337498
Clean, well-run, older-style hotel. Most rooms have private facilities. $

Carthage, Gammarth and Sidi Bou Saïd

LE RESIDENCE (5-star)
La Marsa, Bay of Tunis
Tel: (71) 910171; Fax: 910144
Tunisia's first five-star hotel to rank with an international five star. Member of the 'Leading Hotels of the World'. $$$$

CORINTHIA KHAMSA HOTEL (5-star)
Gammarth, Bay of Tunis
Tel: (71) 911100; Fax: 910041
Beautiful hotel with attractive pool, private beach, excellent restaurant and all amenities. Free shuttle to Tunis and Sidi Bou Saïd.

ABOU-NAWAS-GAMMARTH (5-star)
Gammarth, Bay of Tunis
Tel: (71) 741444; Fax: 740400
In a beautiful setting on the Bay of Tunis. Recently renovated and popular with Tunisians living in France. $$$$

SIDI BOU SAID HOTEL (4-star)
Sidi Dhrif
Tel: (71) 740411; Fax: 745129
Good location, comfort and, rare for Tunisia, style. Also offers a swimming-pool. $$$

PALM BEACH REINE DIDON (3-star)
Rue Mendès-France, Carthage Hannibal
Tel: (71) 733433; Fax: 732599
Close to the museum, with fine views over Carthage and bay. $$$

Jasmine decorates everything

El Haouaria

L'ÉPERVIER (2-star)
Tel: (72) 297017
The best hotel in town, on the main street. Restaurant and bar. $$

DAR TOUBIB (unclassified)
Tel: (72) 297163
Signposted down a series of farm tracks. Bungalows in rural setting. Damp out of season, but pleasant in summer. Rudimentary bathrooms. $

Hammamet

Large hotels line the beaches either side of town. Among these, the **Hammamet Sheraton**, Avenue Moncef Bey (Tel: 72-226271; Fax: 227301), is a firm favourite, but it is 5km (3 miles) from the centre ($$$$).

GRAND HOTEL MERCURE DAR HAYET (5-star)
Route de la Corniche
Tel: (72) 283399; Fax: 280 424
Hammamet-style villa with annexes, beach and pool. $$$$

ROYAL AZUR (5-star)
Avenue Bourguiba
Tel: (72) 278500; Fax: 278999
Part of three hotels, each of different levels but sharing spa facilities. $$$$

HOTEL YASMINA (3-star)
Tel: (72) 280222; Fax: 280593
Central. More character than most with attractive pool and shaded garden. $$$

HOTEL SAHBI (2-star)
Avenue de la République
Tel: (72) 280807; Fax: 280134
Comfortable pleasant rooms. Try to secure one which opens on to the terrace. Good value. $–$$

Bizerte

HOTEL PETIT MOUSSE (2-star)
Route de la Corniche
Tel: (72) 432185; Fax: 438871
Excellent restaurant. Ask for a room with an ocean view. Best to book. $$

Tabarka

HOTEL MEHARI (4-star)
Tel: (78) 670184; Fax: 673943
Part of the Iberotel chain, with plenty of facilities. $$$$

ABOU NAWAS MONTAZAH (3-star)
Tel: (78) 673532; Fax: 673530
New resort-style hotel on the edge of the bay. Good sports facilities. $$$

HOTEL MIMOSAS (3-star)
Tel: (78) 673018; Fax: 673276
Agreeable small hotel. $$$

HOTEL LES AIGUILLES (2-star)
Avenue Habib Bourguiba
Tel: (78) 673789; Fax: 673604
Relative newcomer. Comfortable and reasonably priced. $$

Ain Draham

HOTEL RIHANA (3-star)
Tel: (78) 655391; Fax: 655396
Out of town, to the south. Functional but comfortable. Fine views. $$$

HOTEL BEAU SÉJOUR (unclassified)
Tel: (78) 647005
Ivy-clad hunting lodge/hotel with bags of character but few comforts save for the log fire in reception in winter. $

El Kef

HOTEL SICCA VENERIA (3-star)
Tel: (78) 202388
Clean, but characterless modern building. Doubles as the local drinking den. $$

HOTEL LES PINS (2-star)
Tel: (78) 204300; Fax: 202411
Spacious rooms, nicely furnished, with views over the valley On the northern road leading into the town centre. $$

Dougga/Teboursouk

HOTEL THUGGA (2-star)
Tel: (78) 465713/465800
Modern, small hotel in rural setting. Simple, but comfortable. Restaurant. Half-board recommended. $$

Sousse

Hotels (2-star–5-star) hug the beach between Sousse and Port el Kantaoui. Nearly all of them cater to the package market, but they often have vacancies out of season. Among the best hotels, though a 15-minute taxi ride into the centre, is the 5-star ($$$$) **Diar El Andalous**, Port el Kantaoui (tel 73-246200; fax: 246348), which offers good sports facilities.

Cheaper and more central alternatives:

HOTEL JUSTINIA (3-star)
Avenue Hedi Chaker
Tel: (73) 226381; Fax: 225993
Relatively modest in size. All rooms –

Splendid in its own way

small but comfortable – have balconies. No pool, but bang in front of the beach. Good rates out of season. $$$

HOTEL MEDINA (1-star)
Tel: (73) 221722; Fax: 221794
Basic, but well-run and clean hotel in the medina. Bar, in spite of the hotel's proximity to the Great Mosque. Be aware that when it is busy, staff may not honour bookings. $

Kairouan

HOTEL AMINA (3-star)
Tel: (77) 235466; Fax: 235411
Fairly simple but clea hotel. One of the best of the lack-lustre choices in Kairouan. $$$

HOTEL CONTINENTAL (3-star)
Tel: (77) 231135; Fax: 229900
Opposite the Aghlabid Pools and the tourist office. Unattractive but redeemed by its large swimming-pool (Kairouan is baking hot in summer). $$

HOTEL SPLENDID (3-star)
Rue 9 Avril
Tel: (77) 227522; Fax: 230829
Attractive tiled interior. Dining-room and bar. Tends to fill up with adventure tour groups en route to the south, so best to book. $$$

TUNISIA HOTEL (2-star)
Avenue de la République
Tel: (77) 231855; Fax: 231597
This is a good alternative to Hotel Splendid. Comfortable rooms, with fans and bathrooms. Breakfast area, but no restaurant. $$

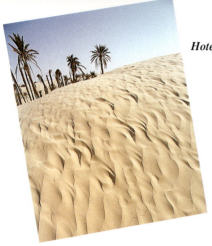

Hotel views at Douz

HOTEL SPLENDID (1-star)
Tel: (76) 450053
Rooms line a courtyard. Basic but friendly and clean. Rooms have fans. Bar. *$*

Tamerza

TAMERZA PALACE (4-star)
Tel: (76) 485322; Fax: 453722
Attractive new hotel with good amenities. *$$*

Douz

HOTEL MEHARI (3-star)
Tel: (75) 471088; Fax: 471589
Striking new hotel on the edge of the dunes. Pool and good restaurant. *$$$*

HOTEL SAHARA DOUZ (3-star)
Tel: (75) 470864; Fax: 470566
Attractive and nicely placed on the edge of the dunes. Swimming-pool. *$$$*

HOTEL SAHARIEN (3-star)
Tel: (75) 471337; Fax: 470339
Well-established, cheaper option, in the middle of the palmerie. *$$$*

HOTEL SABRA (unclassified)
Bab ech Chouahada
Tel: (77) 225095
Basic, cheap, clean. Good location. *$*

Tozeur

TRYP DAR CHERAIT (5-star)
Tel: (76) 454888; Fax: 454472
Oriental architecture. Good facilities. *$$$$*

PALM BEACH SOFITEL (5-star)
Tel: (76) 453111; Fax: 453911
The most luxurious of the new hotels that have been built here in recent years. *$$$$*

HOTEL EL HAFSI (3-star)
Tel: (76) 452558; Fax: 452726
Flashy new hotel near the Belvedere. *$$$*

OASIS DAR TOZEUR (3-star)
Tel: (76) 452522; Fax: 452153
Attractive hotel on the edge of the palmerie. Inviting pool. *$$*

HOTEL EL JERID (2-star)
Tel: (76) 454516; Fax: 454515
Also on the edge of the palmerie. Pool and garden. Good value. *$–$$*

Jerba

The three hotels recommended below are small hotels in Houmt Souk, but if you would rather be by the sea, explore the luxury hotels on the east-coast strip, such as Royal Garden (5-star), tel: 75-745777, fax: 745770; Hasdrubal (5-star), tel: 75-657650, fax: 657730; and Yadis (4-star), tel: 75-747235, fax: 747223.

DAR FAIZA (1-star)
6 Rue de la République
Tel: (75) 650083; Fax: 651763
Comfortable rooms in garden setting, with small pool and tennis court. *$–$$*

HOTEL DES SABLES D'OR (unclassified)
Houmt Souk
Tel: (75) 650423
Tiny hotel occupying old house. Private showers but communal (very clean) WCs. Recommended. *$*

TOURING CLUB DE TUNISIE MARHALA (unclassified)
Houmt Souk
Tel: (75) 650146

East-coast luxury, Jerba

Tunis offers the best nightlife

Old *fondouk* converted into a basic hotel. Shared but clean amenities. *$*

Matmata

HOTEL MATMATA (2-star)
Tel: (75) 230066; Fax: 230177
Not a converted troglodyte dwelling, but probably more comfortable because of it. Restaurant, bar and murky pool.

If you would rather spend the night underground, there are several choices: **Touring Club de Tunisie Marhala**; **Hotel Sidi Driss**; and **Hôtel Les Berbères**. All offer shared but clean facilities.

Tataouine

SANGHO PRÉVILEGE (3-star)
Tel: (75) 860124; Fax: 862177
Slightly out of the centre on the road to Chenini, this is the best accommodation in town. Good restaurant. *$$$*

Ksar Ghilane

PAN-SEA
Tel: (75) 900; Fax: 621872
In the desert southwest of Tataouine. Only accessible by four-wheel drive. Luxurious tents amid the dunes of the Sahara. A special treat. *$$$$*

NIGHTLIFE

Tunis and the resorts offer the best nightlife, though even here it tends to be concentrated in the hotels and is fairly sedate: piano bars, half-empty discos; cabaret and the occasional belly dancer floor show. Hotels often lay on folklore troupes and snake and scorpion charmers to entertain guests, especially in the South, where there is little else to do in the evening.

Tunis's French-built theatre on the corner of Avenue Habib Bourguiba and Rue de Grèce operates in winter only (Oct–June). It runs a varied programme, from classical Western music and *mahlouf* (classical Tunisian) to popular Egyptian song music and plays. To find out what's on, consult *La Presse* or *Le Temps*.

The strip north of Tunis between La Goulette, with its fish restaurants, Sidi Bou Saïd, with its Café des Nattes, and La Marsa, offers the liveliest non-tourist oriented nightlife.

HEALTH & EMERGENCIES

Emergency telephone numbers:
Police: 197
Ambulance: 71-341250/280

Hygiene and Health

Tap water is safe in main cities, but you may prefer bottled water for drinking; use bottled water in rural areas if you are not assured of its purity. Popular brands include Safia and Melliti.

The greatest dangers to health are too much sun, especially when combined with a

heavy intake of alcohol, and contaminated food. If you go down with a stomach upset, drink plenty of bottled water.

In cases of serious diarrhoea or vomiting replace body salts by using a rehydration solution, available at one of the excellent and numerous pharmacies. To find an all-night pharmacy consult newspapers *La Presse* or *Le Temps*.

Doctors (*docteurs*) and dentists (*chirurgiens-dentistes*) are listed in the phone directory. Your embassy will be able to supply a list of doctors who speak your language. Consultations are not expensive. In Tunis, emergency treatment is provided by the Aziza Othmana Hospital (Place du Gouvernement, La Kasbah).

Theft or Loss of Belongings

Any possessions lost or stolen should be reported to the police and a certificate of loss obtained for insurance purposes. Loss or theft of your passport should also be reported to your consulate.

Official Help

Consulates cannot pay medical bills or bail you out if you run out of money, but will contact your family or friends on your behalf and ask them to help. Only in cases of destitution will a consulate make a repayable loan.

COMMUNICATIONS & NEWS

Airmail letters and postcards take about five days to reach Europe and two weeks to the US, Canada and Australia. Buy stamps in PTT (Poste, Téléphone, Télégraphe) offices (see *Business Hours* for opening times).

Telephone

It is possible to make direct international calls from some public call boxes in Tunisia (generally, main cities only) but it's more often necessary to phone through an operator in a PTT office. Dial 00 for an international line, followed by the national code (44 for the UK; 1 for Canada and the US; 61 for Australia; 64 for New Zealand) and then the number you wish to dial, minus any initial zeros.

When looking for a public telephone, look out for signs saying 'Taxi Phone' as well as PTTs and booths.

Newspapers

Several Tunisian newspapers are published in French, including *La Presse*, *Le Renouveau* and *Le Temps*, all pro-government. They are all useful for listing upcoming events, train timetables and all-night pharmacies, as is the weekly English-language *Tunisia News*.

Traditional horseman

Television and Radio

There are four Tunisian channels broadcasting in Arabic and French. In addition, Italian channels can be picked up in the north. Larger hotels receive satellite television. There are many French language radio stations.

LANGUAGE

Spoken languages are Tunisian Arabic and French, but in the resorts basic English and German are often spoken in hotels and restaurants.

SPORT

Golf

To attract upmarket visitors, resources have been ploughed into improving and expanding golfing facilities in Tunisia and the Tunisian Open Golf Tournament has become a major golf tournament.

There are seven courses of good standard: two at Monastir (18 holes), the most beautiful and challenging (designed by Robert Fream); Tabarka (designed by Ronald Fream, 18 holes); two at Hammamet (18 and 9 holes); El Kantaoui (36 holes); and Carthage (18 holes).

Watersports

Waterskiing, windsurfing, sailing, jet skiing, parascending, etc, are available in the resorts. Snorkelling and scuba diving are best off Tabarka on the north coast.

USEFUL INFORMATION/ADDRESSES

Tourist Information Offices

In Tunisia there are National Tourist Offices (ONTT) in all large towns and they are usually complemented by a Syndicat d'Initiatif, which supplies more local information. Offices are always signposted.

Tourist Information Offices Abroad

London: 77A Wigmore Street, London W1H 9LJ. Tel: 020-7224 5561.
Washington: Embassy of the Republic of Tunisa, Tourist Section, 1515 Massachusetts Avenue NW, Washington DC 20005. Tel: (202) 862 1850.

Embassies & Consulates

British: 141–143 Avenue de la Liberté, Tunis. Tel: (71) 793322.
Australia: Affairs are handled by the Canadian Embassy (see below).
US: 144 Avenue de la Liberté 1002, Tunis. Tel: (71) 782566.
Canada: 3 Rue du Sénégal, Tunis. Tel: (71) 796577.

FURTHER READING

Fountains in the Sand by Norman Douglas. (Oxford University Press). A xenophobic but entertaining account of the author's adventures in southern Tunisia at the turn of the century.

Tangier to Tunis by Alexandre Dumas (Peter Owen). The famous author visited Tunis in 1846 at the invitation of the French government. A French warship was put at his disposal.

Salammbo by Gustave Flaubert (Penguin Classics). Novel set in 3rd-century Carthage.

Roman North Africa by E Lennox Manton (Seaby). Highly readable history of the Romans in North Africa.

The Mosaics of Roman North Africa edited by Bernard Ashmole, John Boardman and Martin Robertson (Oxford University Press). Informative study, with plenty on Tunisia's mosaics.

The slow way home

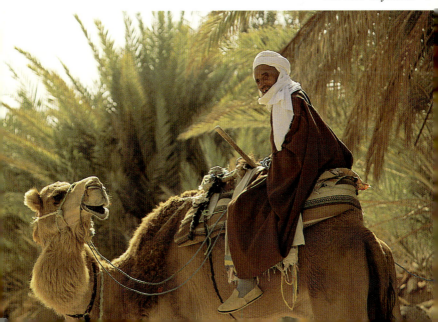

Photography	J D Dallet *and*
Pages 6/7, 26т, 30, 41, 44, 45, 47, 48, 55т, 63, 65, 69, 78	David Beatty
11	Mary Evans Picture Library
Back Cover	Apa Publications/Gary John Norman
Front Cover	Tony Stone Images/Lorne Resnick
Cover Design	Tanvir Virdee
Cartography	Berndtson & Berndtson

INSIGHT
Pocket Guides

The travel guides that replace a tour guide – now better than ever with more listings and a fresh new design

Insight Pocket Guides pioneered a new approach to guidebooks, introducing the concept of the authors as "local hosts" who would provide readers with personal recommendations, just as they would give honest advice to a friend who came to stay. They also included a full-size pull-out map. Now, to cope with the needs of the 21st century, new editions in this growing series are being given a new look to make them more practical to use, and restaurant and hotel listings have been greatly expanded.

Also from Insight Guides...

Insight Guides is the classic series, providing the complete picture with expert and informative text and stunning photography. Each book is an ideal travel planner, a reliable on-the-spot companion – and a superb visual souvenir of a trip. 193 titles.

Insight Maps are designed to complement the guidebooks. They provide full mapping of major destinations, and their laminated finish gives them ease of use and durability. 100 titles.

Insight Compact Guides are handy reference books, modestly priced yet comprehensive. The text, pictures and maps are all cross-referenced, making them ideal books to consult while seeing the sights. 127 titles.

INSIGHT POCKET GUIDE TITLES

NOTES